Published by BSA Publishing 2024 who assert the right that no part of this publication may be reproduced, stored in a retrieval system or transmitted by any means without the prior permission of the publishers.
Copyright Barry Faulkner 2024 who asserts the moral right to be identified as the author of this work
    Proof Reading/Editing BSA
Cover art Orphan Print, Leominster.

. The information in this book is taken from police and court records where available, recorded witness statements, local media reports, the internet, biographies and other reference works. Over time some of the occurrences may have been exaggerated or embellished. Any parts of the book not verified by public record should be treated as allegations. The book is without prejudice.

ALASKA

Capital punishment has never been practiced in Alaska throughout its history as a state, as it was abolished in 1957. Between December 28th, 1869, and April 14th, 1950, between the Department, District and Territory of Alaska twelve felons, all male, were executed by hanging for murder, robbery, and other crimes. Some were European, some were Native American, and two were African. The territorial legislature abolished capital punishment in 1957 during preparations for statehood, making Alaska the first in the West Coast of the United States to outlaw executions, along with Hawaii, which did the same.

THOMAS BUNDAY

Born September 28th, 1948 – committed suicide March 16th, 1983.

Thomas Richard Bunday was born on September 28th, 1948, in Nashville, Tennessee. He was the younger of two children in the family, his elder brother Ralph being 15 years older than him. Bunday spent his childhood and youth in a socially unfavourable situation: his father, a World War 2 veteran, suffered from mental disorders and was aggressive towards both his wife and younger son. After his father died in 1963 Thomas refused to attend his funeral and ran away from home for several days.

Bunday was unpopular among the other children at school, but he was a good student, a sociable child who had many friends and acquaintances, which helped develop his positive outlook on life. After graduating from high school in 1966, he married his high school sweetheart and in 1967 joined the United States Air Force where he achieved the rank of technical sergeant. In the late 1960s and early 1970s, Bunday was serving in Southeast Asia. During this period, his wife gave birth to a son fathered by another man.

Despite this, he continued to live with his wife, who later gave birth to a daughter, but the extramarital child strained their relationship. In the mid-1970s, Bunday was sent to Eielson Base, Alaska. During this period, he began to show signs of emotional burnout and began visiting a psychotherapist.

On June 13th, 1980, 11-year-old Doris Oehring went missing from North Pole, Alaska; they found her bike in a ditch. A witness saw a blue vehicle near the area where the bicycle was found and helped the police create a composite sketch; but no leads were generated. To make matters worse, this was the second known abduction in the area in less than a year. Eight months earlier, on August 29th, 1979, a boy hunting in the woods found the decomposing body of 19-year-old Glinda Sodemann who had been strangled and shot.

Nine months after Doris Oehring mysteriously went missing 16-year-old Wendy Wilson also disappeared. Her friend last saw her talking to a man in a white truck. Wendy's body was found three days later. She had been strangled and shot in the head as well. Police wondered if there was more than one predator and as they scrambled to find leads, another dead body of a woman turned up near Eielson Air Force Base. The victim was identified as 21-year-old Marlene Peters. Marlene was strangled and also shot in the head.

The police were very worried because of the number of murders in one location, and then a fifth woman, Lori King, vanished. Military and civilian search teams failed to find her until one day soldiers out hunting found her body. She too was strangled and shot in the head. Unable to calculate the next move of the serial killer, state troopers tried another tactic. They staked out the killer's dumping grounds that were within a 10 mile radius of Eielson AFB. And then the killings stopped.

In November 1982, troopers received a call from Henrietta, Texas informing them a woman had been murdered in the same distinct way as the victims of their suspected serial killer. Police worked with the military to see if they couldn't narrow down the suspects based on who owned a blue car or white pick-up truck seen at two of the abductions. And finally, they came up with a name: Thomas Richard Bunday. Bunday was a TSgt in the Air Force who transferred to Sheppard AFB shortly after the murder of the fifth victim in Alaska.

Alaska investigators learned Bunday owned a blue car and a white truck, and he was on the Air Force's 'watch' list because there had been several complaints made about his inappropriate sexual remarks to women in the workplace. Alaska investigators also learned Bunday served in the military for fifteen years and was a married father of two.

On March 7th, 1983, Alaska investigators talked to Bunday for three hours about everything but the murders and they did this for several days hoping he would confess; but he refused to talk. Bunday didn't deny the crimes; but refused to confess. After a week of interrogation, the troopers obtained a search warrant for Bunday's property. They found a lot of incriminating evidence that directly tied him to the crime in Alaska but Alaska Troopers had no power of arrest outside of Alaska and they had to obtain an arrest warrant from Alaska. The Governor offered a private leer jet to bring Bunday back to Alaska. The arrest and flight was scheduled for the next day but he failed to show up as promised, made an excuse and another time was booked.

. Instead of meeting with the Alaska investigators again, Thomas Bunday slipped past surveillance at his house on his motorcycle and killed himself. He died by crossing the centre line on a main road and slamming into a truck at 100 mph.

Police had hoped they would get more information from him when they would have charged him in Alaska. They wanted to know where Doris Oehring's body was so they could give the family closure. In August 1986, three years after Bunday died, Doris's skull was found in a remote section of Eielson Air Force Base. It was later learned that

Bunday's technical job in the Air Force most likely allowed him to view his body dump sites via surveillance cameras and relive his sadistic behaviour. Bunday was most likely watching investigators at the crime scene via these cameras. Alaska state investigators are convinced that Thomas Richard Bunday was responsible for the five murders in Alaska. And they believe Bunday denied the murder in Texas to avoid the death penalty before opting instead to kill himself on March 15th, 1983 age 34.

The victims:

Glinda Sodemann, 19, Fairbanks, Alaska (August 29th, 1979)

Doris Oehring, 11, North Pole, Alaska (June 13th, 1980)

Marlene Peters, 21, Tanana, Alaska (January 31st, 1981)

Wendy Wilson, 16, Eielson, Alaska (March 5th, 1981)

Lori King, 18, Fairbanks, Alaska (May 16th, 1981)

Cassandra Goodwin, 22, Henrietta, Texas (never admitted this one)

JASON MICHAEL CODY

Born February 7th, 1978 – sentenced to 99 years in prison August 10th, 2007.

On August 2nd, 2006, a young man went into a gun shop in Juneau and asked the owner, Raymond Coxe, to show him some .22-caliber rifles. Coxe showed the man several and then went into the back of the store. A short time later, one of Coxe's employees told him that the man had left the store, a .22caliber rifle was missing, and there was $200 in cash left on the counter. The price of the missing rifle was $195.
Coxe tried to find the man outside, because he was required to have the man fill out paperwork to legally sell him the rifle. But the man was gone so he reported the incident to the Juneau Police Department.
Two days later, on August 4th, Edward Buyarski and his employee, Alexandra Griffin-Satre, were working outside the Juneau Fred Meyer store. They were talking with Simone Kim, a painter who was working on the same building. A man in a dark rain jacket and pants approached and shot Simone Kim several times in a random act of violence. Buyarski managed to wrestle the gun away from the man, who then ran up a hill behind the store and into the woods. Griffin-Satre called 911.
Juneau Police Department Sergeant Thomas Bates arrived within three to five minutes at approximately 2:44 p.m. He saw Simone Kim lying on the ground. Kim appeared to be gravely wounded and ultimately died from his wounds. The rifle, a sawn-off .22, was also lying on the ground.

Sergeant Bates interviewed Buyarski around 3:00 p.m. and Griffin-Satre around 3:15 p.m. Buyarski and Griffin-Satre explained what had happened. Sergeant Bates stated that the witnesses described the shooter as a white male, approximately six-feet tall. They said that he was wearing dark-coloured rain gear. Buyarski described the rain gear as the non-rubberized kind. They both said that the man ran uphill into the woods behind the Fred Meyer store. Sergeant Bates broadcast the description of the suspect and details of the area where the suspect had fled into.

The Juneau Police Department obtained a helicopter, and Sergeant Bates was flown over the wooded area with a thermal imaging device in an attempt to locate the suspect.

Troy Cunningham lived in a duplex on the hill directly behind Fred Meyer. On the afternoon of August 4th, Cunningham saw "a suspicious-looking person" running near his house. Cunningham thought the man looked "guilty of something" and that the situation "just seemed wrong." Cunningham ran to the window and yelled, "Private property get out." The man turned toward Cunningham and said, "I'm leaving." He saw the man climb a fifteen-foot rock retaining wall. Cunningham described the man as white, around thirty years of age, wearing black light-duty rain gear, with a hood. Cunningham said that the man had short curly hair, with no beard. The man was climbing uphill in the mud, using both his legs and arms like going up a ladder. About five minutes later, Sergeant Paul Hatch knocked on Cunningham's door. Cunningham showed Sergeant Hatch the footpath where the man had gone and a boot print in the mud on the top of the rock wall. Sergeant Hatch asked Cunningham to put a bucket over the boot print to preserve it. Shortly thereafter, other police officers appeared and started measuring and taking pictures of the boot print.

Paola Hannon, Cunningham's tenant and resident of the other unit in his duplex, also noticed the man when she heard Cunningham yell at him. She saw him go uphill into the forest. She described him as white, age twenty-five to thirty. According to Hannon, the man had short brown hair and wore a dark coat, probably black.

Lieutenant Troy Wilson, team commander of the Special Emergency Response Team (SERT), met with Sergeant Hatch around 5:30 p.m. Sergeant Hatch pointed out the footprints behind Cunningham's residence. Three members of SERT, including Lieutenant Wilson, followed "an overgrown trail" where the suspect had been headed. They were looking for a white male, about six feet tall, with a large build, and wearing dark clothing. While investigating a sound in some thick brush, SERT encountered a man running up the path in a dark nylon rain coat and pants. They stopped the man, identified themselves, and asked him why he was there. The man said he was looking for his backpack and eventually identified himself as Coday. SERT confirmed this with identification that Coday had on him. They placed him in handcuffs, walked him back to where Sergeant Hatch was, and turned him over to the uniformed officers waiting there. Lieutenant Wilson stayed in the area. The officers then cleared the area and did not find anyone else in the vicinity, although they did find a tent that they later discovered belonged to Coday. Lieutenant Wilson testified that, given the information that he had, he believed Coday was the person that they were looking for in connection with Simone King's killing.

Sergeant Scott Erickson was the officer in charge of the investigation unit on August 4th, 2006. He responded to the scene of the shooting at about 3:00 to 3:15 p.m. He saw the rifle involved in the shooting, and was able to determine that it matched the rifle that had been illegally obtained from Coxe's gun store. Sergeant Erickson testified that when he saw Coday escorted from the woods that Coday fitted "the totality of information we had gotten based on the descriptions from the witnesses."

Sergeant Erickson made the decision to detain Coday and take him back to the police department. Sergeant Erickson did not want to have witnesses come to the scene, because having them identify Coday while he was standing next to a patrol car in handcuffs might prejudice any future trial or line-ups.

After witnesses later identified Coday from a photo line-up, and after he interviewed Coday, Sergeant Erickson formally arrested Coday at around 6:50 p.m.

Coday's trial began on May 7th, 2007. The prosecution brought forward two Fred Meyer workers as witnesses plus DNA evidence on the gun and Coday's boot prints leading away from the crime scene.

When the guilty of first degree murder verdict was read out Coday head butted his attorney and had to be restrained and led from the court room in handcuffs. He received 99 years for Kim's murder plus two extra for weapons misconduct. He will be eligible for parole in 2046.

As an aside the family of Kim issued a wrongful death lawsuit in 2008 against Coxe alleging that gun smith should have known better than to leave anybody alone in a store with a firearm.

PAUL ELY Jr.

Born 1968 – committed suicide October 7th, 1996.

On October 27th, 1996, Anchorage policeman, Dan Seely, 40, went to deliver a warrant to Paul Ely, 27, on Birdwood Loop after Ely had failed to turn up at a court hearing. Seely had been to the house before on domestic abuse responses.

When he arrived at the house he got no answer, a neighbour yelled that the man he was looking for was at the back door. The front door was locked so Seely ran around to the back of the house. He saw a man and yelled out to him.

"He said he wanted to talk to him," the neighbour said. But the man ran into the apartment block next door where his wife and two small children were staying with a friend. Seely radioed that his suspect was running down a hallway in the block and he was going to go after him.

That was the last radio transmission dispatchers heard from Seely. Neighbours heard a gun shot from inside the building. Investigators believe Ely ran into a back bedroom at the apartment, and when Seely approached the door, he shot him in the face at close range.

After shooting Seely, Ely made his way to where his estranged wife, Christina Ely was holding on to their daughter, Jessica, 5. Ely shot the little girl in the head. The bullet passed through her head and hit the mother in the stomach.

The Elys' 4-year-old son, Corey, was sitting on the neighbour's lap when Ely put a gun to his head and killed him. Ely then put the gun to his own head and shot and killed himself.

Other officers had arrived to hear the final shots. Officer Seely was taken to a local hospital where he died about an hour after being admitted. Ely and his children were all pronounced dead at the scene. Christina Ely, 28, was taken to Providence Medical Centre in serious condition but survived.

Officer Seely was killed just two days before he and his wife, Deborah Walters Seely, would have celebrated their first wedding anniversary. She worked as a dispatcher/call taker and was on duty when her husband was killed. She was expecting a child.

The Elys had a history of domestic problems and recently divorced with Christine getting control of the children. Paul Ely had previously been convicted of beating his wife. She had a protective order barring her husband from coming near her. The warrant officer Seely was carrying charged Ely with violating that court order.

ROBERT CHRISTIAN HANSEN

Born February 15th, 1939 – died in prison August 21st, 2014.

It was during the period from 1971 to 1983, that Robert Hansen stalked the sleazy parts of Anchorage looking for victims. He is known to have killed at least 17 young women, although only 12 bodies were ever found. One report actually estimated the number at 37, and an FBI spokesman commented that Hansen could actually be one of the country's worst serial killers if the truth was ever to come out. Hansen also admitted to about 30 rapes in the same period, and never showed any sign of remorse for any of his crimes.

The case is significant for two reasons. It is the only known killing spree in which many of the women were apparently flown into the wilderness by the killer, released and then hunted down like an animal. It also set a legal precedent in 1983 when psychological profiling was used for the first time as the main basis for issuing search warrants on Hansen's property.

Hansen's killing spree continued for at least 12 years because, instead of people admitting that he was a dangerous sociopath, he was time and time again labelled as an upstanding family man by those who knew him. Appearances can indeed be deceptive.

Robert Christian Hansen was born on February 15th, 1939, in Esterville, Iowa, to a Danish immigrant baker and his wife. His childhood was not easy, as his father was very strict, and Robert worked long hours in their family bakery. As well as being of slight build, Robert had acne so bad that he almost never socialized, and is remembered as a "loner" who had a stuttering problem.

On December 7th, 1960, the first major event occurred that would fit Hansen into the psychological profile of a developing serial killer. As retribution for perceived abuses by the people of Pocahantas, Iowa, he forced a 16-year-old employee at the bakery to help him burn down the school bus garage. Unfortunately for Hansen, then 21, the teen had morals, and confessed to the arson. Hansen was sentenced to 3 years in prison, and his wife of only 6 months divorced him. He served only 20 months of that sentence before being paroled despite having been assessed as having an "infantile personality" which made him obsessive about getting even with people he thought had wronged him in some way.

Within a few months of being released, Hansen had married again. He also started stealing just for the thrill of doing it. Although he was caught several times, no charges were ever made; his father had friends in the right places. In 1967, the Hansens decided it was time for a new start, and left for Alaska.

In the mountains around Anchorage, Hansen honed his skills as a hunter, and in 1969, 1970 and 1971, had 4 animals entered into the Pope & Young hunter's record book. In about 1971 he discovered that another type of hunting satisfied him more; the human kind.

Anchorage at the time had an extremely rough district. Largely run by Seattle Mafia boss Frank Colacurio, it was a wide-open district centred on Fourth Avenue, where anything went. Young women were lured there by promises of making huge wages 'dancing' in clubs with names like Wild Cherry, Arctic Fox, Booby Trap and the Great Alaskan Bush Company. The population and disposable income skyrocketed in Anchorage during the oil boom, with the bigger gambling clubs skimming off $50-$100,000 a month in cash. Between the clubs were peep shows, and magazine stands featuring the worst kind of child pornography. Part of that world was violence - from beatings and armed robberies to firebombs and murders, the police were kept very busy. Between 1979 and 1983, police responded 207 times to disturbances at the Booby Trap club alone.

Inside this unregulated world, Hansen found all the victims he could want - women who, for $300, would go anywhere with him. From his looks and thin physique women apparently felt they had no reason to fear him; as one rape victim reported, "He sort of looked like the perfect dork."

Once they got in his truck the psychopath appeared, and the number of victims grew rapidly over the years. Most of the rapes were never reported, and even when Hansen was positively identified, his respectable facade meant he was always believed over the prostitute's version of the story. In the vastness of Alaska, there were never any witnesses to the murders. He was very careful where he hid the bodies and in 1980 he even shot the dog of a woman he had murdered, so that the dog wouldn't lead anybody to her body in a shallow grave.

In 1977, the courts blew a chance to keep Hansen off the streets for a few years. He had stolen a chain saw, and although psychiatric reports made it clear that he was a danger to society, he served only 1 year of a 5-year sentence before parole. He was ordered to stay on a lithium program to control mood swings for a diagnosed bipolar effective disorder, but that order was never enforced either in prison or after his release. Just a few weeks after his early release, he killed again.

As the body count climbed, his respectable look continued to build. In January 1981, he opened a bakery at 9th and Ingra, using $13,000 from the insurance settlement of a faked burglary at his home. When the fraud was discovered, he claimed that all the 'stolen' wildlife trophies were later mysteriously found in his back yard, and he had just forgotten to tell his insurance company.

In January 1982, he bought a plane, a Piper Super Cub N3089Z - although he never got a pilot's license, it became one of the main tools in his killing spree. He would pick up a woman on Fourth Avenue, handcuff her or tie her up at gunpoint, and fly her out to the Knik River. After landing on a remote sandbar, the naked girl was given a few minutes start before the hunt began. When Hansen flew back to Merrill Air Field, he never had a passenger.

Like many serial killers, Hansen was very methodical. On his aviation chart, he marked many of the locations where he buried his victims. The Knik River was a favourite location - close to town yet remote, with hundreds of solid sandbars to land his plane on. All washed clear of tracks at the next tide.

Hansen was a "trophy collector", another common attribute of serial killers. His living room was loaded with mounts from his legitimate hunts, while his basement was the storage space for the trophies from his human victims. It was largely this human trophy collection that resulted in his successful conviction - among the significant items was a fish necklace that had been custom-made for victim Andrea Altiery.

The turning point in the case occurred in September 1983 when one of Hansen's rape victims agreed to testify. The police hoped that by tying this case in with several others, they could put him away for a few years at least.

The investigation of the disappearing women, which had now brought Hansen into sharp focus, was hampered by attitude problems in both the Anchorage Police Department (APD), and in the DA's office. When an APD officer took his information on the case to the State Troopers, he was bawled out for it. Hansen and his father were still respected members of the community with friends in high places. When the Troopers were trying to draw up documents for searches of Hansen's property, they were told by the DA's office that they had no time to do it - a personal favour brought the Assistant DA from Fairbanks down to do it.

On October 27th, 1983, Hansen's life of prowling the streets of Anchorage at night ended. Armed with several search warrants, police went through the Hansen family's house, cars and his plane, vacuuming, photographing, sketching and seizing evidence. Robert Hansen was arrested and charged with assault, kidnapping, weapons offenses, theft and insurance fraud. Bail was set at a half-million dollars.

Over the next few months, enough evidence was assembled to charge Hansen with 4 murders. As part of a plea bargain, Hansen agreed to show police where the graves of the murdered women were. Only 12 were located.

On February 27th, 1984, Superior Court Judge Ralph E. Moody sentenced Hansen to 461 years plus life, without any chance of parole. He was initially sent to the maximum security facility at Lewisburg, PA, but in 1988 he was returned to Alaska. He became one of the first prisoners in the new Spring Creek Correctional Centre in Seward. He died in prison on August 21st, 2014 age 75.

Although the Pope & Young book publisher initially stated that Hansen's crimes did not invalidate his bow hunting records, they have since removed his name from their record books. Hansen's wife and 2 children tried to remain in Alaska, but after 2 years of having the children harassed at school, Mrs. Hansen filed for divorce and they moved away.

LOUIS D. HASTINGS

Born 1944 – sentenced to 634 years in prison on July 27th, 1984.

Hastings had worked as a computer programmer at Stanford University in the late 1970s. He and his wife left California for Alaska in 1980, initially moving into a duplex in east Anchorage, where he operated a computer services company out of their home. In the summer of 1982, about eight months before the murders, Hastings and his wife bought a vacation home in Kennicott. By the winter of 1982, both Hastings's business and his marriage were failing. He began to spend more and more time alone at the Kennicott cabin, while his wife remained in Anchorage. In Kennicott, Hastings began refining an attack he had been planning for nearly a year.

Hastings had fled the overdevelopment of California for the wilderness of Alaska. Instead he found the state in the throes of development, largely due to the opening of the trans-Alaska oil pipeline, which wynds from Prudhoe Bay south to the port of Valdez on Prince William Sound. The eight hundred mile pipeline cost $8 billion to build, renewed the natural resource economy in Alaska, and now is responsible for transporting 25 percent of the total U.S. oil production.

When he lived in California, Hastings had once volunteered to clean oil-soaked birds following an offshore oil spill. Shortly after he arrived in Alaska, he began to target the pipeline. According to one psychiatric report, Hastings "was disturbed by the population growth and influx of money into the state and determined that the best way to interrupt this was to destroy the pipeline and thus cut off Alaska's wealth and consequent growth." Destruction of the pipeline would be the end to his McCarthy rampage.

It would begin when the weekly mail plane arrived. Hastings would kill anyone who showed up at the air strip for the mail drop, and most of McCarthy's residents usually did. With most of the residents eliminated, Hastings would then hijack the mail plane and kill the pilot. He then planned to land the plane near the pipeline at a pump station about eighty miles west of McCarthy and rig the plane to take off again with no one at the controls. At that point, Hastings would commandeer a fuel truck and ram the pipeline while shooting at it. He theorized that the cold winter weather would congeal the oil in the broken pipeline, thus minimizing environmentally damaging spillage while disrupting the oil flow. The fuel truck would burst into flames, charring his body beyond recognition.

Hastings thought that because the entire town would be dead and his body would be unrecognizable, he could destroy the pipeline and commit suicide without revealing to his family that he had been a murderer and a suicide. Officials would believe he had died, along with the rest of Kennicott and McCarthy, at the hands of an unknown killer.

On March 1st, 1983, Louis Hastings put his plan into operation and attempted to murder everybody living in McCarthy, a small out-back hamlet in Alaska. McCarthy and Kennicott country is severe and unforgiving. Temperatures can fluctuate from 50 degrees below zero in winter to 90 degrees in the summer. Annual snowfall averages 52 inches. Almost 230 miles east of Anchorage, McCarthy and Kennicott are located in the middle of the Wrangell-St. Elias National Park and Reserve.

By 2 P.M. that day, six of McCarthy's dozen or so year-round residents lay dead in and around the air strip and their houses while two more were wounded. One cowered outside a greenhouse, tightly clutching her upper right arm to stem the flow of blood, the other had been flown by a neighbour to Glennallen, a town one hundred miles northwest and home of the nearest hospital and State Troopers, to receive treatment for gunshot wounds to his face and head and alert the Troopers.

The thirty-nine-year-old Louis Hastings had completed his killing headed west on the lone road connecting McCarthy to the outside world. He rode a snowmobile taken from one of his victims. Each of the dead had received multiple gunshot wounds, including at least one single wound to the head.

After killing McCarthy's residents, Hastings set out to sabotage the Alaska pipeline. The plan began to unravel, however, after Hastings's nearest neighbour survived two shots to his head and escaped to warn others.

The previous night, Hastings had played a board game with Chris Richards in Kennicott, a town of just four homesteads about five miles north of McCarthy. Hastings won. During the course of conversation, Richards mentioned that a couple of McCarthy's residents were away on a skiing trip. Hastings seemed disappointed. Richards also warned Hastings about cutting firewood from dead trees on land that had been sold recently and thus might now be off-limits to such activity.

The next morning, at about 8:30am, Richards saw Hastings approach the front of his home from the south side. Richards thought Hastings--large, soft-spoken, balding, and bespectacled with an unkempt red beard--was stopping by on his way to pick up the mail. Richards pushed the outside door ajar and invited Hastings in for coffee. Hastings set down a heavy backpack and, before entering, took a deep breath. Richards turned his back to the door and faced the stove to continue preparing breakfast. Then he began to turn his head to greet Hastings when two shots hit him. One in the face. He managed to push Hastings over and made an escape out into the deep snow in his socks.

He scrambled three-quarters of a mile up a steep hill to a neighbour's unoccupied cabin. Hastings fired several shots at the fleeing Richards, nicking his right arm. At the cabin, Richards got boots, a parka, and snowshoes. From there he stumbled about one-tenth of a mile southwest to the newlywed Nashes' cabin, which was situated on the trail connecting Kennicott to McCarthy. At the cabin, as the Nashes attended to his wounds, Richards told them what had happened. The Nashes said that they had seen Hastings heading towards McCarthy twenty minutes earlier. Richards then insisted that they arm themselves and go to the runway to warn the others who were sure to be congregating there to wait for the mail plane.

The Nashes rode a snow machine, pulling Richards behind in a sled, to the airstrip. At the north end of the airstrip, they met Gary Green, a local pilot and guide who was cleaning snow off one of his planes. Green said that he too had seen Hastings about twenty minutes earlier, heading toward the Heglands' home, Hasting's nearest neighbours.. The Nashes and Green decided that Tim Nash would go check on the Heglands while Green warmed up his plane to fly Richards to Glennallen, about a forty-minute flight away.

After warming up his engine, Green taxied to the end of the runway to load Richards into his plane. Amy Nash then noticed her husband running down the strip approaching them. Green got out of the plane and met Tim Nash on the runway. Tim told Green he had just been to the Heglands'.

There, Tim had smelled a heavy concentration of gunsmoke and saw blood all over the inside of the house. Tim thought that the Heglands were dead and noticed that someone had attempted to clean up the blood in the Heglands' kitchen. While Tim was standing in the kitchen, he saw Hastings on the back porch. Nash fired a shotgun blast at Hastings that struck a doorjamb and Hastings returned fire, striking Tim in the right leg.

Green and the Nashes decided that the Nashes would remain to warn others away from the airstrip while Green took off with Richards to get help. As Green lifted off, he saw Tim and Amy Nash walking toward each other on the east side of the runway. On his way to Glennallen, with Richards bleeding in his back seat, Green contacted the incoming mail plane that was scheduled to land at 11 a.m. and told the pilot not to land in McCarthy. He then radioed the state police in Glennallen.

In the meantime, Hastings had backtracked toward the airstrip along a dog-sled trail. The trail snaked through dense brush behind a large mound of snow across the runway from the Nashes. Hastings crawled atop the mound and, after Green took off, fired at least ten rounds at the Nashes two hundred fifty yards away. The Nashes fell. Hastings walked to within fifty feet of their prone bodies and fired another two shots. He continued to approach the Nashes and fired two more shots from close range into their heads.

Hastings then dragged the Nashes to the top of the snow bank opposite his sniping location to hide them in deeper snow. At about that time, Harley King and Donna

Byram arrived at the north end of the airstrip on King's snow machine. Byram saw Hastings walking over the snow bank on the west side of the airstrip and then saw blood in the snow on the east side. She wondered who would be butchering animals on the runway. As they drew abreast of the Nashes' bodies, Hastings started firing at them. Byram, who was standing on a sled that trailed the snow machine, saw bullets hit King and the snow machine. One bullet hit Byram in her upper right arm. King accelerated the snow machine as more bullets hit it. Travelling south, away from Hastings, King lost control of the snow machine. His leg had been broken by one of Hastings's shots. The snow machine threw King and Byram to the runway near the path that led from the airstrip to the Heglands.

As Byram attempted to load King back onto the snow machine, Hastings approached from one hundred yards away. Byram froze. King told Byram that he couldn't move and that she should save herself. Byram hurried toward the Heglands. As she entered the spruce woods, she heard Hastings shoot King twice. When Byram got to the Heglands, she noticed that the door had been kicked in. She was afraid to enter, so she hid outside the Heglands' greenhouse. After killing King, Hastings began to look for Byram. He approached the Heglands' house, calling out, "One not dead. One not dead." Byram cowered outside the nearby greenhouse, tightly gripping her injured arm. All she heard was Hastings's bootsteps on the Heglands' porch and the wind whipping the Visqueen sides of the greenhouse.

Hastings abruptly ended his search for Byram and sped off on the Nashes' snow machine. His plan was starting to unravel. Hastings thought the police would respond in a fixed-wing aircraft and that, if he got away from the airstrip, he would be safe. However, the first state troopers to respond left Glennallen in an unmarked helicopter. They saw Hastings heading west on snow-covered McCarthy Road. When the troopers landed, Hastings waved and offered no resistance. He said that he was Chris Richards and that Lou Hastings had "gone berserk" and was "shooting up McCarthy." They also had a description of Hastings. Based on the fact that Richards was already in Glennallen receiving treatment for his wounds and based on the description of Hastings that Richards and Green had given them, the troopers arrested Hastings.

Hastings was charged with six counts of first degree murder and on July 27th, 1984, 15 months after the shootings he was sentenced to 634 years in jail.

ISRAEL KEYES

Born January 7th, 1978 –committed suicide in prison December 2nd, 2012.

Israel Keyes was a serial killer, bank robber, burglar, arsonist, kidnapper and sex offender. He murdered at least 3 people and operated between July 2001 and February 2012.

Keyes planned murders long ahead of time and took extraordinary action to avoid detection. Unlike most serial killers, he didn't have a victim profile. He always killed far away from his home, and never in the same area twice. On his murder trips, he kept his mobile phone turned off and paid for items with cash. He had no connection to any of his victims. In the Currier murders, he flew to Chicago, and there rented a car to drive the 1000 additional miles to Vermont. He then used the murder kit he had hidden two years earlier to carry out the murders.

Keyes admired Ted Bundy and shared several similarities with him: Both were heavy drinkers, methodical, intelligent and felt a possession over their victims. However, there are notable differences. Bundy's murders were spread throughout the country, mainly because he lived in many different areas, and not as an intentional effort to avoid detection as was the case with Keyes. Bundy only targeted attractive young women, usually with hair parted down the middle, while Keyes had no particular type of victim.

Keyes specifically went for campgrounds and isolated locations. He claimed to only use guns when he had to and preferred strangulation; this was due to the pleasure he derived from witnessing victims lose consciousness in the struggle. He claimed to not kill children or parents of children, primarily because of his daughter, whom he feared finding out about him and his crimes. However, police and FBI investigators were sceptical of this claim and suspected Keyes of killing several teenagers and children.

Keyes did not admit to any murders during his three years service in the United States Army, but did admit to twice attempting rapes of women whilst enlisted, once with a prostitute while on leave in Egypt, and another time with a college student he met in Israel. He is believed to have resumed his killing spree in 2001 following his discharge. Keyes had ties to New York; he owned 10 acres of land and a dilapidated cabin in the town of Constable. He also confessed to committing bank robberies in New York and Texas. The FBI later confirmed that Keyes robbed the Community Bank branch in Tupper Lake, New York, in April 2009. He also told authorities that he burglarized a Texas home and set it on fire about that same time.

An FBI report stated that Keyes burglarized twenty to thirty homes across the United States and robbed several banks between 2001 and 2012. He is believed to have been responsible for as many as eleven deaths in the United States, and potentially even more victims outside the country.

His possible victims include;

Julie Marie Harris, a 13-year-old Special Olympics medallist in skiing, disappeared on March 2nd, 1996, while waiting for a ride to a local church in Colville, Washington; her remains were found on April 26th, 1997, in a wooded area a few miles away. A cause of death was not determined. Harris was a double amputee whose prosthetic feet were found by the Colville River a month after her disappearance. Keyes, who was then 18 years old, lived in the area at the time and was questioned about her case sixteen years later after he was arrested in 2012, but he neither confirmed nor denied killing her.

Cassandra "Cassie" Emerson, 12, another young girl from the Colville, Washington area, was reported missing after the remains of her mother, Marlene Kay Emerson, 29, were discovered in their burned-out trailer home on June 27th, 1997. Cassie's remains were found in 1998 about thirteen miles from her home. Keyes did admit that his first act of arson was with a trailer in Colville.

Keyes admitted to investigators that he had killed five people in Washington State, and was the subject of an active investigation by the state police and the Federal Bureau of Investigation over a long period of time. Keyes claimed to have either buried or submerged a victim in a lake in Neah Bay, Washington sometime between July and October 2001; a body was found, but the death was ruled accidental. He also confessed to the double murder of a young couple which occurred between 2001 and 2005. According to Keyes, the male was beaten to death and the female was fatally strangled; both victims were buried. Between 2005 and 2006, Keyes said he had killed two further victims separately; saying that one was dumped in Lake Crescent, Washington.

Keyes did not have a Felony criminal record in Washington although he had been stopped on two occasions for minor driving-related offenses. After his arrest authorities reviewed unsolved murder and missing persons cases to determine which, if any, may have been the work of Keyes. In 2012, they identified a possible victim known only as Lewis County Jane Doe, who was a woman found in by a passing motorist in the Peterman Hill area in Morton, Washington on April 7th, 2011. In 2022, the victim was formally identified but her identity was not publicly revealed. Keyes also confessed to at least one murder in New York State. In late 2012, authorities had not determined the identity, age, or sex of that victim, or when and where the murder may have occurred but regarded the confession as highly credible.

Keyes is a suspect in a series of 2007 crimes by the "Boca Killer", near Boca Raton. The first case in the murder series was that of Randi Ann Malitz Gorenberg, 52, who on March 23rd, 2007, was abducted from the Boca Town Centre Mall parking lot. Within an hour her body with two fatal bullet wounds, was dumped at a different location. The second crime was the kidnapping of an unidentified woman who claimed she and her toddler son were abducted from the same shopping mall parking lot on August 7th, 2007. Though the kidnapper wore a mask and sunglasses, the victim caught glimpses of his face and described him as a tall, athletically built man with long hair, which generally matched Keyes's description. This woman was released unharmed after the assailant forced her to withdraw cash from an ATM. The third Boca case was the murder of Nancy Bochicchio, 47 years old, and her 7-year-old daughter, Joey Bochicchio-Hauser, who were found fatally shot in their vehicle at the Boca Town Centre Mall parking lot on December 12th, 2007.

Authorities believe Keyes may have murdered 48-year-old Debra Feldman, a prostitute with alleged substance abuse issues after discovering that he had frequently searched for her missing person's case on his computer shortly before his arrest. Feldman was last seen at her apartment in Hackensac, New Jersey on April 8th, 2009. Her body has never been recovered. Federal agents showed Feldman's image to Keyes upon which he said, "I don't want to talk about her yet." It is suspected that Keyes buried her near Tupper Lake, New York.

On May 28th, 2011, Madison 'Maddy' Geraldine Scott was last seen during the early morning hours at Hogsback Lake near Vanderhoof, British Columbia after attending a party at a campsite. Her remains were found in May 2023. Hogsback Lake is a 33-hour drive from Anchorage, Alaska, where Keyes lived at the time. Keyes chose victims by how unlikely it was that they would be linked to him, and he said on one occasion, "I would let my victims come to me... in some remote location." Keyes travelled to Canada extensively and when he was asked about whether he had killed anyone in Canada, he said, "Canadians don't count."

Keyes confessed to murdering 49 year old William Scott Currier and 55 year old Lorraine Currier of Essex Vermont. Keyes broke into the Currier home on the night of June 8th, 2011, and tied them up before driving them to an abandoned farmhouse where he shot Bill and sexually assaulted and strangled Lorraine. Their bodies have never been found. Two years prior, Keyes hid a "murder kit" near the Currier home, which he later used. After the murders, he moved most of the contents to a new hiding place in Parishville, New York, where they remained until after his arrest.

Keyes' last confirmed victim was 18-year-old Samantha Tessla Koenig, a coffee booth employee in Anchorage Alaska. Keyes kidnapped Koenig from her workplace on February 1st, 2012, took her debit card and other property, sexually assaulted her and then killed her the following day. He left her body in a shed and went to New Orleans, where he left on a pre-booked two-week cruise with his family in the Gulf of Mexico. When he returned to Alaska, he removed Koenig's body from the shed, applied makeup to the corpse's face, sewed her eyes open with fishing line, and snapped a picture of a four-day-old issue of the Anchorage Daily News alongside her body, posed to appear that she was still alive. After demanding $30,000 in ransom, Keyes dismembered Koenig's body and disposed of it in Matanuska Lake, north of Anchorage.

Keyes is a suspect in the murder of 58-year-old James "Jimmy" Lamar Tidwell Jr., an electrician who disappeared in Mount Enterprise, Texas on February 15th, 2012. He was last seen at 5:30 a.m. that day after he had finished working the night shift. During a bank robbery in Azle, Texas on February 16th, 2012, the robber – believed to be Keyes – wore a white hard hat similar to Tidwell's. Tidwell's hair also resembled a dark-haired wig worn by Keyes during the robbery. When interrogated later, Keyes stated that his "wig" was, in fact, human hair. When asked where he had obtained the human hair, Keyes refused to elaborate but said, "You don't have to buy real hair to get real hair."

Having read the book Mindhunter; Inside the FBI Elite Serial Crime Unit assiduously in his youth and continued to meticulously study serial killers, as I mentioned earlier, Keyes idolized Ted Bundy and felt that he shared many similarities with him. Both were methodical and felt as though they possessed their victims despite their difference in victim choice and modus operandi.

He even went as far as to imitate Bundy's court escape and was immediately seized by the security guards. Keyes also admired and studied other serial killers yet actively shunned media attention for his crimes as he was fearful of abuse for his family and being labelled a "copycat" for his admiration of Bundy and the others. Keyes called Dennis Rader a "wimp" for apologizing in court and showing remorse for his crimes and expressed his admiration for serial killers "that haven't been caught."

When asked in an interview about Robert Hansen, Keyes replied enthusiastically, stating, "Yeah, I know all about him," before continuing, "I probably know every single serial killer that's ever been written about. It's kind of a hobby of mine." When FBI agents informed him of the 2012 Aurora, Colorado shooting he inquired as to the status of the shooter. Keyes had also expressed mild interest in the mass murder's perpetrator, James Holmes.

After Koenig's murder, Keyes demanded ransom money and the police were able to track withdrawals from her account as he moved throughout the South Western US During that time, the police controversially refused to release surveillance video of Koenig's abduction. Keyes was arrested by Texas Highway Patrol Corporal Bryan Henry and Texas Ranger Steven Rayburn in the parking lot of the Cotton Patch cafe in Lufkin, Texas, on the morning of March 13th, 2012. Investigators had circulated a lookout bulletin for the suspect's car, which had been photographed at ATMs used to withdraw money from Koenig's account. Keyes's car matched this description. Keyes was stopped after he drove slightly over the speed limit. His vehicle was searched after officers spotted cash stained with bright ink, indicating a dye pack from a bank robbery. Koenig's ATM card and cell phone were also discovered in the car.

Keyes was extradited to Alaska, where he confessed to the Koenig murder. He was indicted in the murder case, and his trial was scheduled to begin in March 2013. While incarcerated, Keyes spoke to investigators several times over a period of months. He cooperated to an extent, confessing to some of his crimes, and stated a wish to be executed within one year. He said he wanted to avoid publicity due to the negative attention his young daughter might face but largely stopped cooperating after his identity was revealed in the media. On Wednesday, May 23rd, 2012, Keyes attempted to escape during a routine hearing. He used wood shavings from a pencil to pick his hand cuffs. US Marshals used a taser to subdue him.

While being held in jail at the Anchorage Correctional Complex on suspicion of murder, Keyes managed to conceal a razor blade in his cell. He was not allowed razor blades, and was under security restrictions which allowed use of an electric razor under supervision.

He died by suicide on December 2nd, 2012, by cutting his wrists after a failed attempt at strangulation with a bed sheet. A suicide note, found under his body, consisted of an "ode to murder" but offered no clues about other possible victims. In 2020, the FBI released the drawings of eleven skulls and one pentagram, which had been drawn in blood and found underneath Keyes' jail-cell bed after his suicide. One of the drawings included the phrase "WE ARE ONE" written at the bottom. The FBI believes the number of skulls correlates with what are believed to be the total number of his victims.

CHARLES LOUMAN MEACH

Born October 1st, 1947 – died in prison December 9th, 2004.

Charles Meach was born in Traverse City, Michigan, to a mother who had schizophrenia. He left home at sixteen to travel and accumulated a long record of minor crimes in the States he passed through to finance his travels.

Meach finally made his way to Anchorage, Alaska, and in 1973 he beat 22-year-old Robert Johnson, who worked as a grocery clerk, to death in Earthquake Park after meeting him in a topless bar. He was charged with murder, found not guilty by reason of insanity after two psychiatrists and a psychologist testified he was a paranoid schizophrenic and was sent to Atascadero State Hospital in California.

In 1980, psychiatrists decided that his illness was in remission and he was returned to Alaska under the supervision of the Alaska Psychiatric Institute. In 1981, Meach worked several jobs and was enrolled at the University of Alaska.

On May 3rd, 1982, armed with a .38 calibre revolver that he said he had bought from a man on the street, he shot four teenagers to death while robbing their campsite in Russian Jack Springs park. They were two 19-year-old boys, one 16-year-old girl and one 17-year-old girl. The teens were planning on going to the movies when Meach shot them in cold blood. A witness recalled seeing a new blue bike near the scene and police checked every bicycle shop in the area until they found one who had recently sold a blue bike. The receipt gave Meach's name and address. When interviewed he confessed to the killings and was charged.

He again pleaded not guilty by reason of insanity, but was convicted and sentenced to 396 years in prison without the possibility of parole — the longest sentence in the state's history.

In response to the shootings, the Alaska Legislature revised the criminal statutes on the sentencing of the mentally ill in Alaska State, adding a new verdict "guilty, but mentally ill" where the convicted serve their time in a mental institution until deemed healthy and then transferred to prison for the rest of their sentence. This revision did not apply to Meach's trial, or consequently his sentence. The legislature also narrowed the definition of insanity and tightened the burden of proof for the basic insanity defence. This resulted in Alaska having one of the strictest conditions for the insanity defence of all US states.

Meach died of natural causes on December 9th, 2004, age 57, in the Cook Inlet jail. He is buried beside his parents in the First Congregational Church Garden in Traverse City, Michigan, plot 285 in the Sunset Garden.

EVAN E. RAMSEY

Born February 8th, 1981- sentenced to 210 years in prison 1998, reduced on appeal to two 99 year prison terms.

When Evan Ramsey was just five years old, his father was imprisoned after a police-standoff, and his mother became an alcoholic. Shortly afterwards his family were forced to relocate around the Anchorage area after their house was set on fire. When Ramsey was seven, the Anchorage Department of Youth and Family Services removed him and his two brothers from his mother's custody and placed them in foster care. Evan was separated from his older brother, John, and lived in eleven foster homes between 1988 and 1991.

Ramsey and his younger brother William were allegedly abused by several foster parents. Evan's younger brother claimed that their foster brothers would pay other children to beat Evan as a sick game.

Evan was adopted with his brother at age 10, and settled in Bethel, Alaska with their foster mother. Evan had suffered from depression since early childhood, and had attempted suicide when he was 10 years old.

Evan was believed to have been frequently bullied at school. According to his friends, he complained of being harassed and teased by other students, even to the extent of only addressing him as "Screech", a character from the TV series Saved by the Bell.

In October 1986, Evan's father Don Ramsey went to the Anchorage Times newspaper office armed with an AR .180-223 rifle and a .44 Magnum revolver, and over 210 rounds of ammunition. While inside the building, Don

Ramsey began taking hostages and was involved in a brief standoff with police until he surrendered. His motive for doing this was because he was angered that the Times refused to publish a political letter he had written. He was sentenced to 10 years in prison, and was paroled less than two weeks before his son Evan carried out a school shooting.

Reports say in the two weeks prior to the incident, over 15 students knew of Ramsey's intention to commit a school shooting, and two actually assisted him. One student named James Randall, taught him how to use a shotgun, and another named Matthew Charles told him of the fame that would come from such an action. Reports say that several students brought cameras to school on the day of the shooting, and many were watching the shooting from a library balcony overlooking the student common area.

On Wednesday morning, February 19th, 1997, sixteen-year-old Evan Ramsey entered Bethel High School with a .12 gauge shotgun hidden under his jacket. Ramsey walked towards the student common area where several students were sitting. At the nearest table sat Joshua Palacios, a fellow high school student, talking with several of his friends. Palacios began to turn around and stand up when Ramsey pulled out the shotgun and shot Palacios in the stomach. Palacios later died from his wounds. Two students who were sitting across from Palacios, were also hit by pellets from the shotgun blast. One of the art teachers at the high school, Reyne Athanas, was in the teacher's lounge when she heard the first gunshot. She entered the hallway and observed Ramsey shooting into the ceiling and Palacios lying on the floor beside another student. During this episode, Ramsey paced up and down the hall several times in a very threatening manner. Athanas and Robert Morris, another school teacher, attempted to convince Ramsey to put the shotgun down and give up. Ramsey then aimed the gun at them, but did not shoot. Ramsey then walked away from Athanas and Morris, heading in the direction of the school's main entrance where the administrative offices were located. Meanwhile, Ronald Edwards, the school principal, had heard that Ramsey was in the school with a gun and had been walking through the school looking for him. Edwards found Ramsey as he was approaching the main office. Ramsey aimed the shotgun at Edwards, and Edwards turned around to run back into the school's office. As Edwards was trying to get back into the office, Ramsey shot him in the back and shoulder. Edwards died in his office from the gunshot wounds.

Minutes after the shooting began, Bethel police officers arrived at the high school. Several officers entered and saw Ramsey standing in the common area with the shotgun. Ramsey saw the officers and fired one round in their direction. After a brief exchange of gunfire, Ramsey put the shotgun down and gave up. According to the officers, as he threw the shotgun down, Ramsey yelled "I don't want to die." Officers were quickly able to detain Ramsey and take him into custody.

A grand jury indicted Ramsey on two counts of first-degree murder, three counts of attempted first-degree murder, and fifteen counts of third-degree assault. The State's theory at his trial was that Ramsey sought revenge against both Palacios and Edwards. The State introduced testimony that Ramsey and Palacios had got into an argument and fight two years before the shooting. The State also introduced a letter found in Ramsey's bedroom following the shooting that indicated Edwards was one of Ramsey's intended victims. The letter read, in part;

'Hi, everybody. I feel rejected. Rejected, not so much alone. But rejected. I feel this way because the day-to-day mental treatment I get usually isn't positive. But the negative is like a cut, it doesn't go away really fast, they kind of stick. I figure by the time you guys are reading this, I'll probably have done what I told everybody I was going to do. Just hope a 12-gauge doesn't kick too hard, but I do hope the shells hit more than one person, because I am angry at more than one person. One of the big assholes is Mr. Ed — Ron Edwards, he should be there. I was told that this would be his last year, but I know it will be his last year. The main reason that I did this is because I am sick and tired of being treated this way everyday. Who gives a fuck about it? Now, I got something to say to all of those people who think I'm strange can suck my dick and like it. Life sucks in its own way, so I killed a little and kill myself. Jail isn't for me ever and wasn't.'

Ramsey's major defence at trial was that he was suicidal and did not form the requisite intent to commit first-degree murder or first-degree attempted murder. According to Ramsey, his intent during the shooting was not to kill anyone but merely to scare the people at the school and force the police to go to the high school and kill him. Ramsey's counsel described Ramsey's actions as "suicide-by-cop."

The jury convicted Ramsey of two counts of first-degree murder, one count of first-degree attempted murder, and fifteen counts of third-degree assault. The jury also acquitted him of two counts of attempted first-degree murder and one count of third-degree assault. Judge Wood sentenced Ramsey to a composite term of 210 years' imprisonment reduced on appeal to two terms of 99 years each to run consecutively. He will be eligible for parole in 2066.

JAMES DALE RICHIE

Born November 4th, 1976 – killed in a shootout with police November 12th, 2016.

James Dale Ritchie was an American serial killer. Throughout 2016, Ritchie killed upwards of five individuals in and around Anchorage, Alaska, most of whom he killed in parks or along cycle paths. He always committed his murders at night, often around midnight or a short time after. Ritchie was killed during a shootout with police officers in downtown Anchorage on November 12th, 2016. Following his death, a Colt Python handgun on his person connected him to the string of murders he had committed over the course of two months.

Ritchie was born on November 4th, 1976. He grew up in Anchorage's Wonder Park neighbourhood and attended East Anchorage High School, where he was a standout athlete. Ritchie scored 1200 on his SAT and was recruited by the West Virginia University (WVU) football team in 1994.

After a semester at WVU, Ritchie dropped out and returned to Alaska, and in 1995 became involved in drug dealing and dog fighting. By 1998, Ritchie had adopted the street name "Tiny". Over the following seven years, Ritchie was arrested a number of times, predominantly for drug-related offenses. He was arrested for the last time in Alaska in 2005, when he was apprehended while committing a home invasion with plastic handcuffs and two handguns in his possession. After serving two years in custody, he lived in Alaska, during which time he acquired a Colt Python handgun.

In 2013, Ritchie lent his handgun to a friend and moved to Broadway, Virginia,, where his parents were living at the time. Save for a pair of moving violations of his parole terms, Ritchie had no court appearances and was observed by the police as being a law-abiding citizen. Following a breakup with his girlfriend, Ritchie returned to Alaska in March 2016. He took back possession of the Colt Python from his friend and moved to Airport Heights where he stayed before moving to Penland Parkway trailer park in Anchorage. Ritchie sought mental health treatment though the Anchorage Police Department (APD) but there is no record as to whether he had received a diagnosis.

Ritchie committed his first two confirmed murders during the early morning hours of July 3rd, 2016, when he shot 20-year-old Brianna Foisy and 41-year-old Jason Netter Sr. Their two bodies were discovered together along a cycle path near Ship Creek by a cyclist at 7:45 a.m. Jason Netter was already known for having extensive run-ins with the police, often regarding his drug-related activity, as well as child support issues with his two daughters, one of whom changed her name. Foisy was homeless and had fallen into substance abuse as well, denying intervention offered by her adoptive mother, Marcella Foisy. The nature of Foisy and Netter's relationship – if any – was not determined or disclosed. On July 5th, the murders were ruled a double homicide by the APD and after reviewing hours of surveillance footage, the APD released images of two unidentified men who were persons of interest for the investigation.

The third recorded murder committed by Ritchie took place 26 days later, on July 29th. Shortly after 3 a.m., Ritchie shot 21-year-old Treyveon-Kindell Thompson multiple times while he was riding his bicycle home from work, between Duben Avenue and Bolin Street in East Anchorage. Three girls who spotted Ritchie lingering in the woods near Bolin Street through their window just prior, heard the gunfire and witnessed him grabbing Thompson's bicycle. Ritchie rode the bicycle away from the scene and brought it to his home, where it was seen but not identified as being involved in a crime by witnesses.

The police arrived at Bolin Street, where they found Thompson, who was pronounced dead at the scene. Under Sergeant Slawomir Markiewicz's direction, witnesses were interviewed and enough testimonials were given that a composite sketch of the suspect – who would later be positively identified as Ritchie – was created. Shortly after Thompson's murder, the Alaska State Crime Lab confirmed that the same murder weapon used in Foisy and Netter's murders was also used in Thompson's murder.

During the early hours of August 28th, Ritchie shot dead 34-year-old Kevin Turner and 25-year-old Bryant De Husson in Valley of the Moon Park. An unidentified female passerby who was walking through the park discovered De Husson's body along the trail at 1:42 a.m. Shortly after arriving, police discovered Turner's bullet-riddled body under the pavilion in the park.

Turner, who suffered from schizophrenia and bipolar disorder, was homeless at the time, having left his state assisted living facilities just recently. De Husson, a notable environmental activist in Anchorage, was thought by his father, Gordon De Husson, to be doing a late-night bicycle ride on his newly bought Schwinn bike to meet a friend when he stumbled upon the fatal encounter between

Ritchie and Turner and was killed. There was no relation between De Husson and Turner. In the police report, the APD noted that very little evidence was left at the scene of the crime. However, the Alaska State Crime Lab confirmed that the weapon used to kill Turner and De Husson had also been used in the earlier homicides.

Recognizing a modus operandi displayed by the string of murders, the APD released an advisory notice for citizens to avoid isolated trails after dark. Following the murders of Turner and De Husson, the FBI was brought in to assist with the investigation. On September 6th, Anchorage Mayor Ethan Berkowitz hosted a press conference that asserted that gang violence was largely responsible for the record-breaking number of murders in the city. He refused to acknowledge the evidence lent credibility to a serial killer theory.

The FBI offered a $10,000 reward leading to the apprehension of the suspect responsible for Thompson's murder, while refusing to comment on any connection to the other murders, due to the concern that acknowledging that a weapon tying all the crimes together would run the risk of prompting the killer to dispose of it. The joint APD and FBI task force subsequently received upwards of 175 tips over the following two months – at least one of which pointed to Ritchie.

Ritchie was killed near the corner of 5th Avenue and Cordova Street in Anchorage during a gunfight with 38-year-old Police Officer Arn Salao and 34-year-old Sergeant Marc Patzke of the APD on November 12th, 2016. Officer Salao, while responding to an unrelated report of an unpaid taxi cab fare, spotted Ritchie walking down the street at 4:30 a.m. Salao pulled up alongside Ritchie and asked for him to stop, presumably to ask him if he had witnessed the taxi crime. Ritchie continued walking, prompting Salao to repeat the question over his megaphone.

Without warning, Ritchie turned, walked towards Salao's vehicle, drew his Colt Python and opened fire on Salao, hitting him six times, which resulted in damage to his bones, intestines and liver. Salao exited his patrol car and returned fire while also engaging Ritchie in a physical confrontation. Simultaneously, Sergeant Patzke of the K9 Unit spotted the confrontation and fired upon Ritchie, who was killed by a number of gunshot wounds. Salao was taken to an area hospital, where he was moved out of the intensive care unit after seven hours of surgery.

Following Ritchie's death, the Colt Python pistol on his person was sent to the Alaska Crime Lab, where it was confirmed to have been the murder weapon responsible for the deaths of Brianna Foisy, Jason Netter Sr., Treyveon-Kindell Thompson, Kevin Turner and Bryant De Husson. The investigative task force had not considered Ritchie a suspect, due to his lack of run-ins with the law over the past ten years.

After seventy-eight hours of investigation and contacting the victims' families, APD Chief Chris Tolley hosted a press conference in which he announced the connection between the homicides and the attempt on Officer Salao's life. Additionally, Lieutenant John McKinnon confirmed that the investigation had previously revealed a connection between the murders, but the task force withheld it from the public out of concern that Ritchie would have disposed of the Colt Python had he realized it was being sought. The weapon, which had been purchased in 1971, was not registered to Ritchie; the original owner was questioned by the APD, with the intent of discovering how it found its way into Ritchie's possession and discovered it had been reported as stolen some time ago.

The police had the murder weapon and now had to link Ritchie to it on each of the murders where it was used. Ritchie was immediately identified as being the assailant responsible for Thompson's murder, due to the witnesses and the identification of his photo identification matching the composite sketch. While the APD continued to collect evidence implicating Ritchie's involvement in the other homicides tied to the Colt Python, the FBI looked to trace Ritchie's activities in Virginia and Nevada prior to returning to Alaska in 2016.

On April 26th, 2017, APD spokesperson Renee Oistad announced that sufficient probable cause was determined to confirm that Ritchie was solely responsible for the five murders and, therefore, a confirmed serial killer. Investigators had traced the Colt Python handgun's whereabouts back to confirm that it had found its way into Ritchie's possession prior to the murders of Foisy and Netter in July 2016. With Oistad's announcement, the cases were closed. A month later, on May 23rd, the Anchorage Police Department released dashcam footage recorded just prior to Ritchie and Salao's confrontation, as well as details pertaining to Ritchie's personal history. His burial details have not been released.

MICHAEL ALAN SILKA

Born August 20th, 1958 – killed in a shoot-out with police May 19th, 1984.

Michael Alan Silka was an American spree killer who is believed to have killed nine people primarily in the small village of Manley Hot Springs in Alaska during May 1984. The spree culminated in a shootout with Alaska State troopers in the Alaskan wilderness in which Silka was shot and killed. The motives for Silka's actions are unknown.

Michael Silka grew up in the northwest suburbs of Chicago. From an early age, he had a love of firearms and the outdoors, and had a history of encounters with the law. In 1975, Silka and another juvenile were apprehended while trying to steal camping gear and weapons from a Des Plaines sporting goods store. That same year, Silka and his brother Steve ran away from high school to the Canadian wilderness, only returning when they ran out of food. In February 1977, four months before graduating from high school, Silka was arrested for carrying an antique black-powder muzzle-loading rifle through a park in the suburbs. He was arrested again for the same offense later that year, was convicted and paid a $100 fine.

Shortly afterwards, Silka enlisted in the United States army, at least partly on the advice of a longtime neighbour, Forman Hurst, who later recalled him as "a good kid, a typical teenager who loved the outdoors. That was his No. 1 ambition, to be outside exploring nature." In 1981, he was stationed at Fort Wainwright, located on the East side of Fairbanks, Alaska, until his discharge the same year. Army records show that Silka was rated an expert marksman with theMl6 rifle and grenade launcher. However, his stay at Fort Wainwright was marked by several run-ins with military police, including an assault charge and an arrest for discharging a firearm in a barracks and he was discharged.

Silka returned to the Chicago area and worked at a number of jobs, mostly in construction work. In November 1982, he was stopped for a minor traffic violation and the officer noticed four weapons — a .44 calibre revolver, a .22 calibre semi-automatic pistol, and two knives — in his car. Silka was charged for weapons possession and with resisting arrest after he refused to exit the squad car after arriving at the station.

He was convicted and spent four days in Cook County Jail. On July 21st, 1983, Silka was arrested on another weapons violation after a South Barrington officer stopped him for speeding, and a .22-calibre rifle was found on the back seat. He made several court appearances, the last on October 26th, but then he skipped his bond and fled to Alaska. A warrant for his arrest was issued on December 20th. According to his younger brother Frank, Silka was then working in Alaska for some time, although he did not know what job his brother held.

Silka became a bearded, 25-year-old drifter, first seen in Alaska in the Chena Ridge section of Fairbanks. On April 29th, 1984, police had questioned Silka about fresh blood on a snow-covered mound at his cabin. At the time, the Alaska State Troopers were under the impression that they were investigating whether Silka himself had been killed after a neighbour reported the blood. Troopers dropped the matter when Silka stuck his head out of his shack and explained that the blood was from a moose hide.

However, Silka's nearest neighbour, Roger Culp, had gone missing the day before. Witnesses reported that Silka and Culp went into Silka's cabin, and later they heard as many as eight gunshots. Apparently, witnesses had not reported the incident immediately. When Troopers obtained the new information, they returned to the cabin on May 8th with a search warrant, but Silka was gone. The red spots on the ground, by this point free of snow, were found to be human blood. At this point, Silka was wanted for questioning about Culp's disappearance, but Troopers had no leads as to his whereabouts

Silka was next seen on Monday, May 14th, 1984, at the end of a 150-mile (240 km) dirt road, Alaska Route 2, in Manley Hot Springs, a tiny mining town of 70 people located west of Fairbanks and deep in the interior of Alaska. He was driving a battered brown and white 1974 Dodge Monaco filled with camping equipment and an aluminium canoe mounted on the roof. Unseen by villagers among the equipment were guns and ammunition. According to one resident, Robert Lee, Silka told the villagers that he planned to settle in the area. Silka described himself to Lee as a "mountain man". The villagers were impressed by Silka's common sense of the wilderness and survival, as well as his marksmanship. He was often seen "hanging around" a boat landing on the Tanana River 3 miles (5 km) outside of town.

Silka had set up a tent at the boat landing and was frequently seen paddling his canoe in the Tanana.

Lee said that on Thursday, May 17th between 2 and 4 p.m., six villagers went to the boat landing, all of whom then disappeared. The disappearances were not noted by the locals until the following day, at which point they contacted Alaska State Troopers in Fairbanks on the Friday night. The wife of one of the missing men gave Troopers Silka's license plate number, and the police then checked and learned he was wanted for investigation of the murder of Roger Culp. Two helicopters, three planes and the Troopers' Special Emergency Reaction Team were sent to Manley at 2 a.m. Saturday, May 19th. At the boat landing, Troopers found blood, believed to be human, and used cartridge casings but no bodies.

A wide helicopter search for Silka along the Tanana began at 2 a.m. At this time of year in Alaska, it was still daylight, so the search proceeded without hindrance. By the late hours of the same day, Silka was found upstream about 25 miles (40 km) southeast of Manley in an unnamed tributary of the Zitziana River, which is itself a tributary of the Tanana, near his own canoe and a motorized boat belonging to one of his victims, Fred Burk. Troopers offered Silka a chance to surrender. Instead, he stepped from behind a tree and fired a Ruger 30-06 calibre rifle at one of the airborne helicopters, penetrating the windshield and striking 34-year-old Trooper Troy L. Duncan of Fairbanks in the head killing him instantly, and injuring Captain Donald Lawrence in the face. Trooper Jeff Hall returned fire with an M16 rifle, firing a burst on automatic from a moving helicopter. Five shots struck Silka and killed him. Troopers at the shootout said it was reminiscent of combat in the Vietnam War.

By June 23rd, 1984, four of the bodies — those of Burk, Lyman Klein, Dale Madajski and Larry Joe McVey — had been recovered from the Tanana River. Burk's body was discovered by his wife, Liller, about 75 miles (120 km) downstream from the scene of the killings. For several months, families and friends of the victims searched the brush choked banks of the Tanana.

A memorial service for the victims was held at the boat landing on Sunday, May 20th. Silka was cremated and his ashes were buried in the Sitka Nationa Cemetery next to the Alaska State Trooper training academy in Alaska at his father's request.

Troopers believe that Silka had only been in Alaska about a month before the shootings. It is believed that he dumped the bodies of his victims into the Tanana in the hopes that they would be swept downstream and not be found. The Tanana is as much as a mile wide and 70 to 80 feet (21 to 24 m) deep, and as the water remains near freezing temperatures, the glacier-fed river is heavily silted, and bodies are likely to remain below the surface. The motives for Silka's actions are unclear.

ROBERT FRANKLIN STROUD.
(The Birdman of Alcatraz)

Born January 28th, 1890 – died in prison November 21st, 1963.

Robert Stroud ran away from home at the age of 13, and by 18 had moved to Juneau, Alaska and begun a relationship with a cabaret dancer named Kitty O'Brien. According to Stroud, on January 18th, 1909, while he was away at work, an acquaintance of theirs, F. K. "Charlie" Von Dahmer, viciously beat O'Brien after she refused him sex. After finding out about the incident that night, Stroud confronted Von Dahmer resulting in the latter's death from a gunshot wound. Stroud went to the police station and turned himself and the gun in. However, according to police reports, Stroud had knocked Von Dahmer unconscious and then shot him at point blank range.

Stroud's mother paid for a lawyer for her son, and he was found guilty of manslaughter on August 23rd, 1909 and sentenced to 12 years in the federal penitentiary on Puget Sound's McNeil Island. As Alaska was not at that time a state with its own judiciary, Stroud's crime was handled in the federal system.

During his incarceration Stroud was one of the most violent prisoners at McNeil Island. He assaulted a hospital orderly who had reported him to the administration for attempting to obtain morphine through threats and intimidation, and also reportedly stabbed a fellow inmate who was involved in the attempt to smuggle the narcotics in. On September 5th, 1912, Stroud was sentenced to an additional six months for those attacks and transferred from

McNeil Island to the federal penitentiary in Leavenworth, Kansas.

On March 26th, 1916 he was reprimanded by a guard in the cafeteria for a minor rule violation. Although the infringement was not a serious one, it could have annulled Stroud's visitation privilege to meet his younger brother, whom he had not seen in eight years. Stroud flew into a rage, and stabbed the guard to death. He was convicted of murder and sentenced to be executed by hanging on May 27th, and ordered by the court to await his death sentence in solitary confinement. The sentence was thrown out in December by the U.S. Supreme Court, because the trial jury had not said that it intended for Stroud to hang. In a second trial held in May 1917, he was also convicted, but received a life sentence. That sentence was also thrown out by the Supreme Court on constitutional grounds. Stroud was tried a third time starting in May 1918, and on June 28th he was again sentenced to death by hanging. The Supreme Court intervened, but only to uphold the death sentence, which was scheduled to be carried out on April 23rd, 1920.

Stroud's sentence was again commuted to life imprisonment after Stroud's mother appealed for clemency to President Woodrow Wilson. Leavenworth's warden, T. W. Morgan, strongly opposed the decision to let Stroud live given his reputation for violence. He persuaded Wilson to stipulate that Stroud spend the rest of his life in solitary confinement.

While at Leavenworth, Stroud found injured sparrows in the prison yard and kept them. He started to occupy his time raising and caring for those birds, soon switching from sparrows to canaries, which he could sell for supplies and to help support his mother. Soon Leavenworth's administration changed and the prison was then directed by a new warden who embraced the possibility of presenting Leavenworth as a progressive rehabilitation penitentiary and furnished Stroud with cages, chemicals, and stationery to conduct his ornithological activities.

Visitors were shown Stroud's aviary and many purchased his canaries. Over the years, he raised nearly 300 canaries in his cells and wrote two books, Diseases of Canaries, and a later edition, Stroud's Digest on the Diseases of Birds, with updated specific information. He made several important contributions to avian pathology, most notably a cure for the hemorrhagic septicaemia family of diseases. He gained respect and also some level of sympathy in the bird-loving field.

Soon Stroud's activities created problems for the prison management. According to regulations, each letter sent or received at the prison had to be read, copied and approved. Stroud was so involved in his business that his letters alone required a full-time prison secretary. Additionally, most of the time his birds were permitted to fly freely within his cells. Due to the great number of birds he kept, his cells were dirty and Stroud's personal hygiene was reported to be suffering greatly. In 1931, an attempt to force Stroud to discontinue his business and get rid of his birds failed after Stroud and a female pen friend, Della Mae Jones, made his story known to newspapers and magazines and undertook a massive letter- and petition-writing campaign that climaxed in a 50,000-signature petition being sent to the President. The public complaints resulted in Stroud being permitted to keep his birds in a second cell given to him in which to house them — but his letter-writing privileges were greatly curtailed.

In 1933, Stroud advertised in a publication to publicize the fact that he had not received any royalties from the publisher for the sales of Diseases of Canaries. In retaliation, the publisher complained to the warden and, as a result, proceedings were initiated to transfer Stroud to Alcatraz, where he would not be permitted to keep his birds. Stroud, however, discovered a legal clause which stipulated that he would be allowed to remain in Kansas if he were married there. He then married his friend Della Jones in 1933, which infuriated not only prison officials, who would not allow him to correspond with his wife, but also his mother, who refused any further contact with him. However, Stroud was able to keep his birds and his canary-selling business until it was discovered, several years later, that some of the equipment Stroud had requested for his lab was in fact being used as a home-made still to distil alcohol.

The result was that Stroud was transferred to Alcatraz on December 19th, 1942, While there, he wrote two manuscripts: Bobbie, an autobiography, and Looking Outward: A History of the U.S. Prison System from Colonial Times to the Formation of the Bureau of Prisons. A judge ruled that Stroud had the right to write and keep such manuscripts, but upheld the warden's decision of banning their publication. After Stroud's death the transcripts were delivered to his last attorney, Richard M. English of California.

In 1943, he was assessed as a psychopath, with an I.Q. of 134.

Stroud spent six years in segregation and another 11 confined to the hospital wing. He was allowed access to the prison library and began studying law. He began petitioning the government that his long prison term amounted to cruel and unusual punishment. In 1959, with his health failing, Stroud was transferred to the Medical Centre for Federal Prisoners in Springfield, Missouri. His attempts to be released were unsuccessful. On November 21st, 1963, the day before the assassination of President John F. Kennedy, Robert Franklin Stroud died at the Springfield Medical Centre at the age of 73, having been incarcerated for the last 54 years of his life, of which 42 were in solitary confinement. He had been studying French near the end of his life.

Robert Stroud is buried in Masonic Cemetery, Metropolis, Massac County, Illinois.

ALASKA LADIES

LISA DONLON

Born 1973 – found not guilty of murder on April 3rd, 2013.

In 2010 Lisa Donlon, a mother of three, 37, was charged with second-degree murder, manslaughter and criminally negligent homicide.

She shot her husband, Jason Donlon, once in the head and five times in the back with a .45-calibre handgun while he slept on Oct. 7th, 2010 before calling 911 to report the shooting.

The defence argued Jason Donlon had been raping and torturing his wife for three days. They say he was keeping her against her will in a 12ft x 12 ft cabin or storage shed in Butte, about 40 miles northeast of Anchorage.

Prosecutors argued the killing was non-confrontational, and they said that while medical records showed evidence of scrapes and bruises there was nothing to indicate Lisa Donlon had been tortured.

A grand jury initially declined to indict Donlon but reconsidered after prosecutors presented new evidence.

Her lawyer argued that she was a victim of domestic violence and the shooting was justified.

'I think anyone would have done what Lisa Donlon did to protect herself and to protect her children under those circumstances,' said defence attorney Zachary Renfro during his closing arguments. 'Lisa Donlon was kept in a 12 by 20 cabin against her will, unable to leave by the threat of death to her and death to her children.'

The Donlons married in South Carolina in 1995, and court papers show they had troubles in their marriage when they were living in Eagle River in 2006. That year she obtained a restraining order against her husband and doctors documented her injuries.

In a petition for the restraining order, she said her husband became enraged when she announced she wanted a divorce.

"He packed his things, told the kids `bye," she wrote. "Twenty minutes later he came back with his two loaded guns. He was trying to force me to call the police because he wanted to be shot by police officers so it wouldn't look like a suicide."

She wrote that her husband had pointed a gun to her chest before, and had thrown her out of the house with no clothes on -- an event she said was witnessed by one of their sons. She also stated that her husband had choked her unconscious on one occasion.

She said she didn't call police because she was too scared.

'I have a feeling that he would use his guns easily, and I don't want to create any situation that would trigger that,' she said.

Two days after she obtained the restraining order, Jason Donlon, who was a computer technician for the Alaska Army National Guard, filed for divorce, seeking custody of the children.

They reconciled but the abuse continued and got worse until on October 7th, 2010 she snapped and shot him whilst he slept. Her defence attorney said that she acted in self-defence and that Jason Donlon tortured, kidnapped and raped Lisa Donlon during a three-day period prior to the shooting.

A Palmer jury acquitted Donlon of all charges including second-degree murder, manslaughter and criminally negligent homicide and she walked free from the court.

JANE RETH

Born March 20th, 1964 – sentenced to 36 years in prison March 3rd, 2011.

A former Oswego woman who killed her husband and disposed of his body 23 years before in Alaska made the mistake of confiding her murder to her second husband and then later on divorcing him.

Jane Reth, 46, pleaded guilty to second-degree murder in November 2010 in the 1988 death of her husband Scott Coville. Reth was known as Jane Limm while living in the Fox Valley, before her arrest by Kendall County sheriff's deputies at her Oswego apartment in January 2010.

She was sentenced to 36 years in prison at a trial that followed an investigation by an Alaskan cold case team after her second husband had told a church worker, helping him with their marriage annulment, of his wife's confession to murdering her first husband. That church worker passed the information onto the police in Alaska. Reth's attorney at her trial asked for a sentence of 15 years, saying Reth was seeking "redemption" for her crime, through good works in the Oswego area, and mission work abroad for the Seventh-day Adventist Church.

In her remarks to the court before sentencing, Reth said:

"I don't know that I could say anything that would make anything better. I do know I'm very sorry for what I've done. I thought about it for a very, very long time, and I've thought about what I could say today. There isn't a whole lot I can say."

Reth said she wished she had taken opportunities to get help when she was having problems in her marriage to Scott Coville, and cited her lack of maturity at the time.

In handing down the sentence, George said he found no evidence that domestic violence was a factor, and that the murder was among the more serious types of its kind.

He said Reth showed a level of calculation and callousness by chopping up Coville's body with an axe, putting body parts into garbage bags and disposing of them in several trash bins in Sitka.

"You did nothing to relieve the anguish of friends and family," George said.

The judge cited Reth's lies about Coville's whereabouts to his family, and the fact that she sent a Mother's Day card to Coville's mother a few weeks after the murder, signing it "Scott and Jane." George also took note that Reth later sent a multi-page letter to Reta Coville, his mother, blaming Scott for problems in the marriage, partly due to his use of marijuana.

Troopers also obtained supporting evidence with the cooperation of Christopher Reth. He allowed a phone conversation with his estranged wife, in which she admitted the murder, to be tape-recorded for use as evidence against her, prosecutors said.

Reth was arrested by Kendall County deputies in January 2010 at her apartment in the 2500 block on Light Road in Oswego.

Prosecutors said she confessed to shooting Coville with a .357 Magnum handgun as he slept in their bedroom. She said she chopped up the body on the bed with "a long-handled axe." In her statement to the troopers she said she disposed of the body parts, and the bloody mattress, in trash bins.

Twenty three years after the murder Jane Reth, now 47, was sentenced on March 3rd, 2011 to 36 years in prison after pleading guilty to second degree murder. None of Scott Coville's body parts have been recovered.

ARKANSAS

Capital punishment is a legal penalty in the U.S. State of Arkansas. The verdict must be delivered by a jury and be unanimous. The method of execution was changed from hanging to the electric chair in 1913. The chair was constructed from wood taken from the old gallows. A new chair was installed in the 1970s. The current method of execution is by lethal injection. Executions are currently performed at the Arkansas Department of Correction Cummins Unit situated adjacent to death row in the Varner Unit. The female death row is located in McPherson Unit. The last person executed as of 2024 was Kenneth Williams in 2017.

CHARLES JASON BALDWIN

A.K.A. The West Memphis Three

Born April 11th, 1977 – sentenced to life imprisonment without parole on March 21st, 1994.

This is one of the most involved serial murder cases I have come across. It twists and turns many times and at the end you'll still be left wondering, 'did they or didn't they?' Stick with it to the end.

Charles Jason Baldwin is one of the three members of what has become known as the West Memphis 3 (Baldwin, Damien Echols, and Jessie Misskelley . The three were convicted of killing eight-year-olds Steve Branch, Christopher Byers, and Michael Moore at Robin Hood Hills, West Memphis, Arkansas, on May 5th, 1993.

Baldwin was arrested on June 3rd, 1993 age 16. He was tried jointly with Echols age 17, while Misskelley age 16 was tried separately and testified implicating Baldwin and Echols). The jury convicted both defendants of murder. Baldwin received a life sentence without the possibility of parole.

As of 2020, Baldwin, Arkansas Department of Correction number103335, was in the Maximum Security Unit. He was received by the state prison system on March 21st, 1994.

In 2000, work began on developing evidence that would support an "actual innocence" claim. In 2001, Baldwin filed a motion to have evidence properly preserved and made available for DNA testing, and requested a hearing on the issue. After a lengthy delay, in 2003, the court entered an Order for Preservation of Evidence, without holding a hearing.

On 4th November 2010 the Arkansas Supreme Court ordered a lower-court judge to examine whether the three inmates should be exonerated in light of new DNA evidence. DNA from the crime scene was tested in 2008, and the results of the tests "conclusively excluded Echols, Baldwin and Misskelley as the source of the DNA evidence tested," the Supreme Court wrote in its ruling. The justices also said the lower court must examine claims of misconduct by the jurors. The Justices also ordered new evidentiary hearings for Miskelley and Echols.

****

The West Memphis Three is the name given to three teenagers who were tried and convicted of the murders of three eight-year-old boys in West Memphis, Arkansas in 1993 by a prosecution team that put forth the idea that the only motive in the case was that the slayings were part of a Satanic ritual.

Damien Echols was sentenced to death, Jessie Misskelley, Jr., was sentenced to life imprisonment plus 40 years (he received two 20-year sentences in addition to the life sentence), and Jason Baldwin was sentenced to life imprisonment.

In July 2007, new forensic evidence was presented in the case, including evidence that none of the DNA collected at the crime scene matched the defendants, but did match Terry Hobbs, the stepfather of one of the victims, along with DNA from a friend of Hobbs' whom he had been with on the day of the murders.

The status report jointly issued by the State and the Defence team on July 17th, 2007 states, "Although most of the genetic material recovered from the scene was attributable to the victims of the offenses, some of it cannot be attributed to *either the victims or the defendants*." On October 29th, 2007, the defence filed a Second Amended Writ of Habeas Corpus, outlining the new evidence.

In September 2008, Judge David Burnett (Circuit Court) denied Echols' application for a hearing on the new DNA evidence. The Arkansas Supreme Court heard oral argument on Burnett's decision on September 30th, 2010.

On November 4th, 2010, the Arkansas Supreme Court ruled that Burnett's interpretation of the DNA statute was too narrow and reversed and remanded all three cases for hearings as to whether new trials should be ordered.

Three eight-year-old boys (Stevie Branch, Michael Moore and Christopher Byers) were reported missing on May 5th, 1993. The first report to the police was made by Byers' adoptive father, John Mark Byers, around 7:00 pm. The boys were last seen together by a neighbour, who reported that they had been called by Terry Hobbs, the stepfather of Steve Branch around 6:00pm. Hobbs later denied seeing the boys at all on May 5th. Initial police searches made that night were limited. Friends and neighbours also conducted an impromptu and unsuccessful search that night, which included a cursory visit to the location where the bodies were ultimately found.

A more thorough police search for the children began around 8:00 am on the morning of May 6th, aided by Crittenden County Search and Rescue personnel, along with several others. Searchers canvassed all of West Memphis, but focused primarily on Robin Hood Hills, where the boys were reported last seen. Despite a human chain making a shoulder-to-shoulder search of Robin Hood Hills searchers found no sign of the missing boys. Search and Rescue personnel broke for lunch at 1:00 pm, but police and others continued searching.

Around 1:45pm, Juvenile Parole Officer Steve Jones spotted a boy's black shoe floating in a muddy creek that led to a major drainage canal in Robin Hood Hills. A subsequent search of the ditch found the bodies of the three boys. They were stripped naked and had been hogtied with their own shoelaces: their right ankles tied to their right wrists behind their backs, the same with their left limbs. Their clothing was found in the creek, some of it twisted around sticks that had been thrust into the muddy ditch bed. The clothing was mostly turned inside-out; two pairs of the boys' underwear were never recovered. Christopher Byers also had deep lacerations and injuries to his scrotum and penis, most likely caused by post-mortem animal predation.

The original autopsies were inconclusive as to time of death, but the Arkansas medical examiner determined that Byers died of blood loss, and Moore and Branch drowned. A later review of the case by a medical examiner for the defence determined that the boys had been killed between 1:00 am and 5:00 am on May 6th, 1993.

The official interpretation of the crime scene forensics for the case remains controversial. Prosecution experts claim Byers' wounds were the results of a knife attack and that he had been purposely castrated by the murderer; defence experts claim the injuries were more probably the result of post-mortem animal predation. Police suspected the boys had been raped or sodomized; later expert testimony disputed this finding despite trace amounts of sperm DNA found on a pair of pants recovered from the scene. Police believed the boys were assaulted and killed at the location they were found; critics argued that the assault, at least, was unlikely to have occurred at the creek.

Christopher Byers was the only victim with drugs in his system; he was prescribed Ritalin in January 1993, as part of an attention-deficit disorder treatment. The dosage was found to be at sub-therapeutic level, which is consistent with John Mark Byers' statement that Christopher Byers may not have taken his prescription on May 5th, 1993.

Stevie Branch was the son of Steve and Pam Branch, who divorced when he was an infant. Pam was awarded custody, and Steve was allowed visitation with the boy only when Pam was also present. She later married Terry Hobbs. When Stevie was murdered, his biological father owed over $13,000 in child support, and was under investigation for state tax violations.

Christopher Byers was born to Melissa DeFir and Ricky Murray. After divorcing Murray, Melissa married John Mark Byers, who later adopted her two sons. John Mark Byers had a long criminal history, including charges for making "death threats" against his first wife, and multiple drug and theft offenses. John Mark Byers was a frequent paid informant for the West Memphis Police Department (WMPD), and, when the boys were murdered, was under Federal investigation for suspected grand theft from the U.S. Postal Service. The elder Byers admitted whipping Christopher with a belt only a few hours before the boys went missing, because Christopher had tried to break into his own home. Christopher was not allowed a house key, and the empty house was locked when he arrived home after school. According to Crittenden County Prosecutor John Fogelman, police and other officials suspected John Mark Byers of committing the murders the day the victims were discovered.

Michael Moore was the son of Todd and Dana Moore. Of the three murdered boys, Michael's parents were the only ones still married and who never had any serious criminal charges or investigations made against them.

At the time of their arrests, Jessie Misskelley was 17 years old, Jason Baldwin was 16, and Damien Echols was 18.

Baldwin and Misskelley had previous records for minor juvenile offenses of vandalism and shoplifting, respectively and Misskelley had a reputation for being hot-tempered and engaging in frequent fistfights. Misskelley and Echols had dropped out of high school, but Baldwin earned above-average grades and due to encouragement from a school counsellor, was considering studying graphic design in college.

Echols and Baldwin were close friends, due in part to their similar tastes in music and fiction, and due to a shared distaste for the prevailing cultural climate of West Memphis, which was politically conservative and strongly Evangelical Christian. Baldwin and Echols were acquainted with Misskelley from school, but were not close friends with him.

Echols' family was poor, with frequent visits from social workers, and he rarely attended school. His tumultuous relationship with an early girlfriend culminated when the two ran off together. After breaking into a trailer during a rain storm, they were arrested, though only Echols was charged with burglary.

Police heard rumours that the young lovers had planned to have a child and sacrifice the infant in a satanic ritual; based on this story, they had Echols institutionalized for psychiatric evaluation. He was diagnosed as depressed and suicidal, and was prescribed the antidepressant imipramine. Subsequent testing demonstrated poor math skills, but also showed that Echols ranked above average in reading and verbal skills.

Echols spent several months in a mental institution in Arkansas, and afterwards received "full disability" status from the Social Security Administration. During Echols' trial, Dr. George W. Woods testified for the defence that Echols suffered from:

"... serious mental illness characterized by grandiose and persecutory delusions, auditory and visual hallucinations, disordered thought processes, substantial lack of insight, and chronic, incapacitating mood swings."

At the time of his arrest, Echols was working part-time with a roofing company and expecting a child with his new girlfriend, Domini Teer.

Early in the investigation, the WMPD briefly regarded two other West Memphis teenagers as suspects. Chris Morgan and Brian Holland, both with drug offense histories who had abruptly departed for Oceanside, California four days after the bodies were discovered. Morgan was presumed to be at least casually familiar with all three murdered boys, having previously driven an ice cream truck route in their neighbourhood.

Arrested in Oceanside on 17th May 1993, Morgan and Holland both took polygraph exams administered by California police. Examiners reported that both men's charts indicated deception when they denied involvement in the murders. During subsequent questioning, Morgan claimed a long history of drug and alcohol use, along with blackouts and memory lapses. He furthermore claimed that he "might have" killed the victims but quickly recanted this part of his statement on legal advice.

California police sent blood and urine samples from Morgan and Holland to the WMPD, but there is no indication WMPD investigated Morgan or Holland as suspects following their arrest in California. The relevance of Morgan's recanted statement would later be debated in trial, but was eventually barred from admission as evidence.

The sighting of a black male as a possible alternate suspect was implied during the beginning of the trial, at which time the possibility of conviction of the initial suspects seemed slim. According to local West Memphis police officers, on the evening of 5th May 1993, at 8:42 pm, workers in the Bojangles' restaurant about a mile from the crime scene on a direct route through the bayou where the children were found in Robin Hood Hills reported seeing a black male "dazed and covered with blood and mud" inside the ladies' room of the restaurant. Defence attorneys later referred to this man as "Mr. Bojangles."

The man was bleeding from his arm and brushed against the walls. The man had defecated on himself and on the floor. The police were called, but the man left the scene. Officer Regina Meeks responded by inquiring at the drive through window about 45 minutes later. By then, the man had left and police did not enter the restroom on that date.

The following day, when the victims were found, Bojangles' manager Marty King, thinking there was a possible connection between the bloody, disoriented man and the killings, called police twice to inform them of his suspicions. According to legal testimony during the Echols/Baldwin Trial, after the second telephone call, police gathered evidence from the restroom.

Investigators wore their same shoes and clothes from the Robin Hood Hills crime scene into the Bojangles restaurant bathroom, conceivably contaminating that scene. Police detective Bryn Ridge later stated he lost the blood scrapings taken from the walls and tiles of the restroom. A hair identified as belonging to an African-American male was later recovered from a sheet which was used to wrap one of the victims.

Not surprisingly there has been widespread criticism of how the police handled the crime scene. Misskelley's former attorney Dan Stidham cites multiple substantial police errors at the crime scene, characterizing it as "literally trampled, especially the creek bed." The bodies, he said, had been removed from the water before the coroner arrived to examine the scene and determine the state of rigor mortis, allowing the bodies to decay on the creek bank, and to be exposed to sunlight and insects.

The police did not telephone the coroner until almost two hours after the discovery of the floating shoe, resulting in a late appearance by the coroner. Officials failed to drain the creek in a timely manner and secure possible evidence in the water. The creek was sandbagged after the bodies were pulled from the water. Stidham calls the coroner's investigation as "extremely substandard."

There was a small amount of blood found at the scene that was never tested and no blood was found at the actual crime scene, indicating that the location where the bodies were found was not necessarily the location in which the murders actually happened. After the initial investigation, the police failed to control disclosure of information and speculation about the crime scene.

According to Mara Leveritt, investigative journalist and author of Devil's Knot, "Police records were a mess. To call them disorderly would be putting it mildly." Leveritt speculated that the small local police force was overwhelmed by the crime, which was unlike any they had ever investigated. Police refused an unsolicited offer of aid and consultation from the violent crimes experts of the Arkansas State Police, and critics suggested this was due to the WMPD officers being investigated by the Arkansas State Police for suspected theft from the Crittenden County drug task force evidence room. Leveritt further noted that some of the physical evidence was stored in paper sacks obtained from a supermarket, with the supermarket's name pre-printed on the bags, rather than in containers of known and controlled origin.

Leveritt also mistakenly presumed that the crime scene video was shot minutes after Detectives Mike Allen and Bryn Ridge recovered two of the bodies, when in fact the camera was not available for almost thirty minutes afterwards.

When police speculated about the assailant, the juvenile probation officer assisting at the scene of the murders theorized that Echols was "capable" of committing the murders, stating "it looks like Damien Echols finally killed someone."

One expert in the film Paradise Lost 2: Revelations, stated that human bite marks could have been left on at least one of the victims. However, these potential bite marks were first noticed in photographs years after the trials and were not inspected by a board-certified medical examiner until four years after the murders. The defence's own expert testified that the mark in question was not an adult bite mark, which is consistent with the testimony of the list of experts put on by the State who had concluded that there was no bite mark. The State's experts had examined the actual bodies for any marks and others conducted expert photo analysis of injuries. Upon further examination, it was concluded that if the marks were bite marks, they did not match the teeth of any of the three convicted.

Police interviewed Echols two days after the bodies were discovered. During a polygraph examination, he denied any involvement. The polygraph examiner claimed that Echols' chart indicated deception. However, when asked to produce the record of the examination, the examiner indicated that he had no written record.

On 10th May 1993, four days after the bodies were found, Detective Bryn Ridge questioned Echols, asking Echols to speculate as to how the three victims died. Ridge's description of Echols' answer is abstracted as follows:

He stated that the boys probably died of mutilation, some guy had cut the bodies up, heard that they were in the water, they may have drowned. He said at least one was cut up more than the others. Purpose of the killing may have been to scare someone. He believed that it was only one person for fear of squealing by another involved.

At trial, Echols testified that Ridge's description of the conversation, which was not recorded, was inaccurate. At the time that Echols had allegedly made these statements, police thought that there was no public knowledge that one of the children had been mutilated more severely than the others. This contradicted John Mark Byers, the stepfather of victim Christopher Byers, statement to reporters only minutes after the three bodies were found, "that two boys had been badly beaten and that the third had been even worse." At that time, Det. Gitchell had not released that information. Gitchell later said he had told John Mark Byers some details of the scene first, before the official release to the media. Leveritt also demonstrates that the police leaked some information, and that partly accurate gossip about the case was widely discussed among the public.

Throughout the course of the trial and afterwards, many teenagers came forward with statements regarding being questioned and polygraphed by the local police. They said that Durham, among others, was at times aggressive and verbally abusive if they did not say what was expected of them. After the test, when asked what he was afraid of, Echols replied, "The electric chair."

After a month had passed with little progress in the case police continued to focus their investigation upon Echols, interrogating him more frequently than any other person; however, they claimed he was not regarded as a direct suspect but a source of information.

On 3rd June police interrogated Jessie Misskelley Jr. Misskelley, whose IQ was reported to be 72, making him borderline mentally retarded, was questioned alone; his parents were not present during the interrogation. Misskelley's father gave permission for Misskelley to go with police, but did not explicitly give permission for his minor son to be questioned or interrogated and not told this would be so. Misskelley was questioned for roughly twelve hours; only two segments, totalling 46 minutes, were recorded. Misskelley quickly recanted his confession, citing intimidation, coercion, fatigue, and veiled threats from police.

During Misskelley's trial, Dr. Richard Ofshe, an expert on false confessions and police coercion and Professor of Sociology at UC Berkeley, testified that the brief recording of Misskelley's interrogation was a "classic example" of police coercion. Critics have also stated that Misskelley's "confession" was in many respects inconsistent with the particulars of the crime scene and murder victims, including, for example, an "admission" that Misskelley "watched Damien rape one of the boys." Police had initially suspected that the boys were raped due to their dilated anuses, but forensic evidence later proved conclusively that the murdered boys had not been raped at all, and their dilated anuses were a normal post-mortem condition.

Subsequent to his conviction, a police officer alleged that Misskelley had confessed to her. However, once again, no reliable details of the crime were provided.

Misskelley was a minor when he was questioned, and although informed of his rights, he later claimed he did not fully understand them. The Arkansas Supreme Court determined that Misskelley's confession was voluntary and that he did, in fact, understand his rights warning and its consequences. Misskelley specifically said he was "scared of the police" during his first confession. Portions of Misskelley's statements to the police were leaked to the press and reported on the front page of the Memphis Commercial Appeal newspaper before any of the trials began.

Shortly after Misskelley's original confession, police arrested Echols and his close friend Baldwin. Eight months after his original confession, on February 17th, 1994, Misskelley made another statement to police with his lawyer Dan Stidham in the room continually advising him not to say anything. Misskelley ignored this advice continually and went on to detail how Damien and Jason abused and murdered the boys, while he watched until he decided to leave. Misskelley's attorney, Dan Stidham, who was later elected to a municipal judgeship, has written a detailed critique of what he asserts are major police errors and misconceptions during their investigation.

Vicki Hutcheson, a new resident of West Memphis, would play an important role in the investigation, though she would later recant her testimony, stating her statements were fabricated due in part to coercion from the police.

On 6th May 1993, the day the murder victims were found, Vicki Hutcheson took a polygraph exam by Detective Don Bray at the Marion Police Department to determine if she had stolen money from her West Memphis employer. Hutcheson's young son, Aaron, was also present, and proved such a distraction that Bray was unable to administer the polygraph. Aaron, a playmate of the murdered boys, mentioned to Bray that the boys had been killed at "the playhouse."

When the bodies proved to have been discovered near where Aaron indicated, Bray asked Aaron for further details, and Aaron claimed that he had witnessed the murders committed by Satanists who spoke Spanish. Aaron's further statements were wildly inconsistent, and he was unable to identify Baldwin, Echols or Misskelley from photo line-ups, and there was no "playhouse" at the location Aaron indicated.

A police officer leaked portions of Aaron's statements to the press contributing to the growing belief that the murders were part of a satanic rite.

On or about 1st June 1993, Hutcheson agreed to police suggestions to place hidden microphones in her home during an encounter with Echols. Misskelley agreed to introduce Hutcheson to Echols. During their conversation, Hutcheson reported that Echols made no incriminating statements. Police said the recording was "inaudible", but Hutcheson claimed the recording was audible.

On 2nd June 1993, Hutcheson told police that about two weeks after the murders were committed, she, Echols and Misskelley attended an esbat in Turrell, Arkansas. Hutcheson claimed that, at the esbat, a drunken Echols openly bragged about killing the three boys. Misskelley was first questioned on 3rd June 1993, a day after Hutcheson's esbat confession. Hutcheson was unable to recall the esbat location, and did not name any other participants of the purported esbat.

Hutcheson was never charged with theft. She later claimed she implicated Echols and Misskelley to avoid facing criminal charges and to obtain a reward for the discovery of the murderers.

Misskelley was tried separately, and Echols and Baldwin were tried together in 1994. Under the "Bruton rule", Misskelley's confession could not be admitted against his co-defendants and thus he was tried separately. They all pleaded innocent.

On February 5th, 1994, Misskelley was convicted by a jury of one count of first-degree murder and two counts of second-degree murder. The court sentenced him to life plus 40 years in prison. His conviction was appealed and affirmed by the Arkansas Supreme Court. On March 19th, 1994 Echols and Baldwin were found guilty on three counts of murder. The court sentenced Echols to death and Baldwin to life in prison.

In May 1994, the three appealed their convictions. The convictions were upheld on direct appeal. In 2007, Echols petitioned for a retrial based on a statute permitting post-conviction testing of DNA evidence due to technological advances in DNA made since 1994 which might provide exoneration for the wrongfully convicted. However, the original trial judge, Judge David Burnett, has disallowed hearing of this information in his court. Why?

John Mark Byers, the adoptive father of victim Christopher Byers, gave a knife to cameraman Doug Cooper, who was working with documentary makers Joe Berlinger and Bruce Sinofsky while they were filming the first Paradise Lost feature. The knife was a small utility-type knife, manufactured by Kershaw. According to the statements given by Berlinger and Sinofsky, Cooper informed them of his receipt of the knife on December 19th, 1993. After the documentary crew returned to New York, Berlinger and Sinofsky reported to have discovered what appeared to be blood on the knife. HBO executives ordered them to return the knife to the West Memphis Police Department. The knife was not received at the West Memphis Police Department until January 8th, 1994.

Byers initially claimed the knife had never been used. Blood was found on the knife and Byers then stated that he had used it only once, to cut deer meat. When told the blood matched both his and Chris' blood type, Byers said he had no idea how that blood might have gotten on the knife. During interrogation, West Memphis police suggested to Byers that he might have left the knife out accidentally, and Byers agreed with this. Byers later stated that he may have cut his thumb. Further testing on the knife produced inconclusive results, due in part to the rather small amount of blood, and because both John Mark Byers and Chris Byers had the same HLA-DQα genotype.

John Mark Byers agreed to, and subsequently passed, a polygraph test during the filming of Paradise Lost 2: Revelations, in regards to the murders, but the documentary indicated that Byers was under the influence of several psychoactive prescription medications that could have affected the test results. During the filming of the show, Byers also volunteered his false teeth when presented with the challenge he had bit the boys' bodies, although at the time of the murders he had his original teeth, which he later had voluntarily extracted, and later claimed there was a medical reason for the procedure.

As documented in Paradise Lost 2, Echols, Misskelley and Baldwin submitted imprints of their teeth after their imprisonment that were compared to apparent bite-marks on Steve Branch's forehead, initially overlooked in the original autopsy and trial. No matches were found.

According to the film, John Mark Byers had his teeth removed in 1997—after the first trial. He has never offered a consistent reason for their removal; in one instance claiming they were knocked out in a fight, in another saying the medication he was taking made them fall out, and in yet another claiming that he had long planned to have them removed so as to obtain dentures.

After an expert examined autopsy photos and noted what he thought might be the imprint of a belt buckle on Byers' corpse, the elder Byers revealed to the police that he had spanked his stepson shortly before the boy disappeared. He also had a 1988 conviction for death threats that arose from an incident involving his ex-wife, Sandra Byers. Melissa Byers had contacted Christopher's school a few weeks before the murders, expressing concerns that her son was being sexually abused.

A fact not revealed until after the trial was that John Mark Byers had acted as a police informant on several occasions. His prior conviction for the 1988 incident had been expunged in May, 1992, upon the completion of probation, despite the fact that other criminal charges against him should have caused the revocation of his probation.

In October 2003, Vicki Hutcheson, who played a part in the arrests of Misskelley, Echols and Baldwin, gave an interview to the Arkansas Times in which she stated that every word she had given to the police was a lie. She further asserted that the police had insinuated if she did not co-operate with them they would take away her child. She noted that when she visited the police station they had photographs of Echols, Baldwin, and Misskelley on the wall and were using them as dart targets. She also claims that an audio tape the police claimed was "unintelligible" and which they said was eventually lost, was perfectly clear and contained no incriminating statements. However, Hutcheson did not testify at the Echols/Baldwin trial.

In 2007, DNA collected from the crime scene was re-tested after advances in DNA profiling. None was found to match DNA from Echols, Baldwin or Misskelley. In addition, a hair "not inconsistent with" Terry Hobbs, stepfather to Stevie Branch, was found tied into the knots used to bind one of the victims. The prosecutors, while conceding that no DNA evidence ties the accused to the crime scene, said that, "The State stands behind its convictions of Echols and his co-defendants." without explaining why?

On 29th October 2007 papers were filed in federal court by Damien Echols' defence lawyers seeking a retrial or his immediate release from prison. The filing cited DNA evidence linking Terry Hobbs the stepfather of one of the victims, to the crime scene, and new statements from Hobbs' now ex-wife. Also presented in the filing is new expert testimony that the "knife" marks on the victims were the result of animal predation after the bodies had been dumped.

On 10th September 2008 Circuit Court Judge David Burnett denied the request for a retrial, citing the DNA tests as inconclusive. That ruling was appealed to the Arkansas Supreme Court, which heard oral arguments in the case on September 30th, 2010.

In July 2008, it was revealed that Kent Arnold, the jury foreman on the Echols/Baldwin trial, discussed the case with an attorney prior to the beginning of deliberations and advocated for the guilt of the West Memphis Three as a result of the inadmissible Jessie Misskelley statements. Legal experts have agreed that this issue has the strong potential to result in the reversal of the convictions of Jason Baldwin and Damien Echols. If their convictions are reversed, the State is expected to retry them.

In October 2008, Attorney (now Judge) Daniel Stidham, who represented Jessie Misskelley in 1994, testified at a post-conviction relief hearing. Stidham testified under oath that, during the trial, Judge David Burnett approached the then deliberating jury in the Misskelley matter at approximately 11:50 a.m. and advised them they would be breaking for lunch. When the foreman answered "we may almost be done", Judge Burnett responded "well, you'll still have to return for sentencing." When the foreman then asked "what if we find him not guilty?" Judge Burnett had closed the door without answering. Stidham testified that his failure to request a mistrial based on this exchange was ineffective assistance of counsel and that Misskelley's conviction should therefore be vacated.

On November 4th, 2010 the Arkansas Supreme Court ordered a lower judge to consider whether newly-analyzed DNA evidence might exonerate three men convicted in the 1993 murders of three West Memphis Cub Scouts. The justices also said a lower court must examine claims of misconduct by the jurors who sentenced Damien Echols to death and Jessie Misskelley and Jason Baldwin to life in prison.

In early December 2010, Circuit Court Judge David Laser was selected to replace David Burnett, who was elected to the state Senate, as judge in the appeal hearings.

The families are divided on the belief that the West Memphis Three are guilty. In 2000, the biological father of Christopher Byers, Rick Murray, described his doubts on the West Memphis Three website. In August 2007, Pamela Hobbs, the mother of victim Steven Branch, and John Mark Byers, adoptive father of Christopher Byers, joined those who have publicly questioned the verdicts, calling for a reopening of the verdicts and further investigation of the evidence.

In late 2007, John Mark Byers, adoptive father to Christopher Byers, announced that he now believes that Echols, Misskelley, and Baldwin are innocent. "I believe I would be the last person on the face of the earth that people would expect or dream to see say free the West Memphis 3," said Byers. "From looking at the evidence and the facts that were presented to me, I have no doubt the West Memphis 3 are innocent."

In 2010, district Judge Brian S. Miller ordered Terry Hobbs, the stepfather of victim Stevie Branch, to pay $17,590 to Dixie Chicks singer Natalie Maines for legal costs stemming from a defamation lawsuit he filed against the band. Miller dismissed a suit Hobbs filed over Maines' remarks at a 2007 Little Rock rally implying he was involved in killing his stepson. The judge said Hobbs had voluntarily injected himself into a public controversy over whether three teenagers convicted of killing the three 8-year-old boys had been wrongfully condemned.

Two films, Paradise Lost: The Child Murders at Robin Hood Hills and Paradise Lost 2: Revelations, have documented this case and were strongly critical of the verdict. The movie marked the first time Metallica allowed their music to be used in a movie and drew attention to the cases. The directors are planning two more sequels.

In addition, there have been a few books, including Blood of Innocents by Guy Reel and Devil's Knot by Mara Leveritt, which also argue that the suspects were wrongly convicted. In 2005, Damien Echols completed his memoir, "Almost Home, Vol 1," offering his perspective of the case.

In August of 2011at court, Misskelley, Baldwin, and Echols entered into an Alford plea, which meant they acknowledged there was enough evidence to convict them but that they could continue to assert their innocence. They were sentenced to time served, and the West Memphis Three were all released from prison.

Where are the West Memphis Three now?

It's been nearly 13 years since they became free men again, and they're all now in their mid 40s. Echols is a firm believer in black magic, and he's written books about how it saved his life when he was in prison. His ex-girlfriend Domini Teer, was also pregnant with his son, Damien Seth, when he was arrested. He wed Lorri Davis in 1999, who had written to him while he was in prison.

Baldwin has since moved to Texas, where he co-founded Proclaim Justice, which helps the wrongfully convicted. He's also said that the HBO documentary, Paradise Lost, is likely the main reason why the West Memphis Three were released from prison. He believes that it helped others see the lack of evidence tying the then-teenagers to the case.

Not much is known about Misskelley's life in the years since he was freed. In 2017, he was arrested after a series of traffic violations, but he was not returned to prison. Reports have also surfaced that he's since been working in construction. The three do not appear to be in contact with one another.

HOYT FRANKLIN CLINES

Born 1957 – executed by lethal injection in Arkansas on 3rd August 1994.

On March 25th, 1981, Donald Lehman, his wife, Virginia, and their daughter, Vicki, were at their home when four men wearing ski masks rang the doorbell and forced their way inside. The intruders shot Lehman three times and severely beat him with a motorcycle drive chain in front of his family killing him. The intruders stole more than $1,000 and several guns before making off, according to court documents.

All four men – James William Holmes, Hoyt Franklin Clines, Michael Orndorff, and Darryl Richley were arrested later that same day – they were later tried jointly for capital murder and aggravated robbery. All of them were found guilty and sentenced to death. Orndorff later had his sentence overturned on appeal, and Lehman's family agreed to a life sentence in his case. The other three were all executed one by one on August 3rd, 1994. It was the first triple execution in the United States in the post-Gregg v Georgia modern era.

.After the U.S Supreme court rejected arguments they were being treated like "hogs at a slaughter", Clines, Richley, and Holmes were all executed by lethal injection on August 3rd, 1994. Beginning at 7 pm., the executions by lethal injection took place about an hour apart in a small concrete-block room at the Cummins Unit of the state prison system. Hoyt Franklin Clines, 37, then Darryl V. Richley, 43, and finally, James William Holmes, 37, were each in turn strapped onto the same gurney to be carried to the death chamber and injected with a fatal mixture of chemicals. All three of them declined to make final statements. Clines was executed first, and was pronounced dead at 7:11 p.m. Richley was pronounced dead 58 minutes later, followed by Holmes at 9:24 p.m.

JOHNIE MICHAEL COX

Born 1947 – executed by lethal injection in Arkansas February 16th, 1999.

It was a chilly November 1st, 1989, when Cox, 42, went to Marie Sullens's apartment to kill her. He had chosen that date, All Saints Day, because he thought she would go to Heaven if she died on that day. Sullens was married to Cox's grandfather. He later told police that he had killed Sullens because he suspected that she was trying to kill his grandfather.

When he arrived at her apartment, he found Sullen's friends, Margaret and William Brown were there visiting. Shortly after he arrived, Cox threatened William Brown with a .22 pistol and ordered him to tie up Sullens and Margaret Brown with duct tape. Cox then tied up William himself and bound all three together at the neck. He first tried to sedate the three victims with sleeping medication. Because the drug took too long to take effect, he stabbed the victims and also attempted to shoot Margaret Brown.

Later, unhappy with the delayed effect of the stabbing, Cox attempted to strangle the three victims and then set fire to the house. All three individuals died as a result of stab wounds and injuries from the fire enduring long and painful deaths. Margaret Brown died before the fire as a result of fourteen stab wounds and strangulation. William Brown had wires around his neck and two stab wounds, but died in the fire. Sullens had six stab wounds, some penetrating her lungs, but also died in the fire.

Cox was quickly arrested and confessed in detail, in writing and on videotape, to the murders. He was tried and sentenced to death. After his trial, he filed a motion for a new trial, alleging that his trial counsel was ineffective. After a hearing, the trial court denied the motion.

He appealed both his conviction and the denial of his motion for a new trial to the Arkansas Supreme Court. He raised essentially the same issues in state court that he raised before. The Arkansas Supreme Court denied the appeal

Cox told his spiritual adviser that he was immune to the poisons used in state executions. He wasn't and was executed by lethal injection on February 16th, 1999.

DON WILLIAM DAVIS

Born November 23rd 1962 – sentenced to death March 6th, 1992

Don Davis was a prolific burglar and on October 12th, 1990 broke into the home of Richard and Jane Daniel. Using a .44 Magnum revolver he had stolen in a previous robbery he shot Jane once in the head killing her. Richard Daniel found his wife's body in the basement of the house when he came home from work.

Friends of Davis became suspicious of him being the killer and alerted police who searched his Bentonville rooms and found the revolver and packets of KOOL brand cigarettes, the stub of one had been found at the crime scene. Other items identified as coming from the Daniel's home were also recovered.

Davis was arrested in Las Vegas and charged with the murder. Witnesses testified he had stolen property from the Daniel's home and others told police that the Magnum was kept wrapped in a towel in his car. The bullet that killed Jane Daniels was from that gun.

Davis was sentenced to death on March 6th, 1992. After many appeals and two dates set for his execution it was stopped by Court Appeal Stays and he still sits on death row. His appeals have been exhausted but no execution date set at this time. Davis has given media interviews where he says the state should not execute him as he is a totally different person to the one that killed Jane Daniels. His lawyers argue that he has intellectual disabilities and never been subjected to a proper mental health evaluation.

In 2018 Davis had an altercation with an officer that resulted in others being summoned and Davis producing a razor blade with which he slashed his own throat. He was stabilized at the local hospital and survived the suicide attempt.

Arkansa had planned to execute eight inmates in 2017, including Davis, over an 11 day period but ultimately only four were actually executed before the states supply of midazolam ran out. Midazolam is a sedative used in the lethal injection process. The state has since found a supply of that drug but is lacking another of the three drugs it uses for executions.

DAMIEN WAYNE ECHOLS

Born December 11th, 1974 – sentenced to death but later released.

One of the WEST MEMPHIS THREE

See under JASON BALDWIN

BARRY LEE FAIRCHILD

Born 1952 – executed by lethal injection in Arkansas August 31st, 1995.

Whoa!! This case breaks all the lines of proper law and police conduct with the legal system turning a blind eye.

It was the kind of crime that inflames local passions: the kidnap, rape and murder of a 22-year-old, white Air Force nurse described as "a good Christian girl;" a former homecoming queen and cheerleader raped and murdered by one or more African-Americans. It was the kind of crime for which, in the not too distant past, a black suspect might well have been lynched. But in Little Rock, Arkansas, in 1983, things were different. Or were they?

On the evening of February 26th, 1983, a state trooper gave chase to a car belonging to Marjorie "Greta" Mason. In North Little Rock, the car screeched to a halt and two black men got out and ran. The following morning, Mason's partially nude body was found near an abandoned farm house. Public outcry was immediate and furious. Tommy

Robinson, the local sheriff who would be elected to Congress the next year, went on the air to denounce the crime and promise swift justice.

Six days later, after the media had reported many details of the crime, the police received a tip from an unnamed informant, a man described in police files as inaccurate about half the time and with a tendency to exaggerate. The names he gave the police were the brothers, Robert and Barry Lee Fairchild.

Barry Fairchild was arrested outside a house surrounded by Pulaski County Sheriff's deputies. As he emerged, unarmed, 30 to 50 police surrounded him. He fell to the ground as he was told to do and the deputies released their dog. Fairchild was badly bitten on the neck, side and head. It required seven stitches to close the gap on his head. After being treated at the local hospital for the bites, he was taken to the police station for questioning.

Within a very short time, Barry Fairchild, functionally illiterate and mentally retarded, confessed on camera. He told them he had participated in the crime, but did not actually kill Ms. Mason. He said he was outside an abandoned farmhouse sitting in Mason's car when his accomplice raped her and then shot her twice in the head inside the farmhouse. In important details, Fairchild's confession did not add up.

Before the night was over, Fairchild confessed again on videotape. This time, his confession was at variance with the first in many respects, but was amazingly consistent with what the police knew of the crime.

The discrepancies in the confessions were not the only problems with the case. Fairchild, for example, named his accomplice but later maintained that the name was supplied to him by his police interrogators. Subsequently, it was learned that the man he named was in Colorado at the time. None of the fingerprints found in the car or on Marjorie Mason's belongings could be identified as Fairchild's. A local store owner identified a hat found near the body as belonging to Fairchild. Yet, none of the hair found in it was his. Semen found on Mason's body was blood type O, while Fairchild is blood type A. But none of this seemed to matter. The police had a confession and with a confession they could get a conviction. When the brother, Robert Fairchild, was questioned, he insisted he knew nothing of the crime. He was never charged or fingerprinted.

During the trial, Barry Fairchild recanted the confessions, saying that he had been threatened and beaten by Sheriff Tommy Robinson himself and Major Larry Dill. He testified that when he told the police he knew nothing of the crime, Robinson hit him on the head with the barrel of a shotgun and Dill kicked him in the stomach repeatedly. He said he had been rehearsed for twenty minutes on what to say. This rehearsing seems to be correct as at one point on the videotape, he is asked how many times Mason was raped. He pauses, looks behind the camera, waits with his mouth open and then finally raises two fingers. He looks back at the camera and says, "Two, two times."

The jury believed the sheriff and gave a guilty verdict. District Attorney, Chris Raff, prosecuting his first murder trial as an elected official, said he didn't think anything less than death would be appropriate for Fairchild. The jury believed that, too. On August 2nd, 1983, they sentenced Barry Fairchild to die by lethal injection.

And that might have been the end of it. For seven years, lawyers for Fairchild fought the system and tried in vain to obtain the evidence to prove his contention that the false confessions were beaten out of him. Finally, they received an anonymous call telling them that they were crazy if they thought Barry Fairchild was the only black suspect subjected to the kind of brutality he alleged at the hands of Tommy Robinson, who was by then Congressman Robinson. The caller gave names. The lawyers investigated. What they found was unbelievable.

Numerous other "suspects" had been brought in for interrogation one by one before they brought in Fairchild for questioning. None of them brought in because of a verified link to the crime or car. But, they all had one thing in common: they were all African-American. The lawyers stated that all but one *"were subjected to horrifying brutality. They were beaten... several were bloodied... they were threatened with guns, often thrust into their faces, and they were kicked. All were pushed and shoved and knocked around. They were terrorized racially, threatened with hanging and with being killed and thrown in the river. They were called 'nigger.' ...And they were all told, 'we know you were involved, we know you raped and killed that nurse, we're gonna' do to you what you did to her if you don't tell us what happened.'"*

A petition for habeas corpus relief was filed in the U.S. District Court seeking to invalidate Fairchild's confessions on the basis that they had been coerced. A number of the men subjected to this governmental third degree testified at an evidentiary hearing in August, 1990. Some were too afraid to speak publicly.

Frankie Webb was arrested at his home at 3 in the morning several days after the murder. He testified: *"Sheriff Tommy Robinson and three deputies... tried by force to get me to sign a confession that was already written out. They called me 'nigger' and threatened to kill me if I did not sign it. I refused...the three deputies hit me numerous times over the head with a telephone book... Robinson pulled a .38 revolver from his holster. He held it between my eyes and again threatened to kill me if I did not sign the confession. He cocked the gun. I was afraid and was about to sign... when he pulled it back and... I saw that there was no bullet in the chamber, so I again refused."*

Five deputies showed up at the home of Nolan McCoy three days before Fairchild's arrest. At the sheriff's office, *"Captain Bobby Woodward turned and pulled a gun out and jammed it into my forehead. He said 'Nigger, you know you done raped that nurse. Now you better tell the truth or I'm going to blow your fuckin' head off.' I could see his finger on the trigger, and I thought he was going to kill me. I grabbed his arm and got hold of the gun. It was then that I saw the gun was empty."*

While they were working Nolan McCoy over, they were also working to get a confession from Randy Mitchell. According to McCoy, *"I saw Mitchell in the other room. He looked like he had been beaten bad, and he was crying. His eyes were so swollen that they were almost shut."*

Mitchell was then placed in a holding cell. Charles Pennington, who was put into the same cell, told the court: *"Randy Mitchell was sitting on the bench in the cell. He appeared to have been beaten. His eyes were swollen and his lip had been split and was puffy and had been bleeding. I asked him what happened. He said, 'They whipped my ass.'"*

Donald Lewis became the next suspect. *"During the course of being questioned,"* he told the court, *"...I was physically and verbally abused, as well as threatened because I wouldn't confess to a crime that I did not commit. I surrendered samples of blood, saliva, and hair from my body to the police."*

Not all the testimony of abuse came from the victims. Former deputy sheriff Frank Gibson testified that he had witnessed choking, beating and threats by Sheriff Robinson against Barry's brother, Robert, shortly before Barry Fairchild's arrest. He testified that Sheriff Robinson drove Robert to a wooded area, threw him on the ground, and threatened to kill him if he didn't confess.

According to the former deputy, "Tommy Robinson and Larry Dill wouldn't come out and say, 'go back out there and whup him,' you know, 'go back there and hit him in the head.' Robinson would say, 'You know what I mean. Go on and do what you need to do. I want a confession. You know what I mean.'"

But, like the others, Robert Fairchild didn't confess. And finally, they got hold of Barry Fairchild.

The sheriff's department had tried to coerce confessions from at least five other people in the two or three days preceding Mr. Fairchild's arrest. The same kind of coercion directed toward Mr. Fairchild--physical abuse, brandishing weapons and threatening death--was directed toward the other five suspects as well. But, in the words of one of his appellate attorneys, Richard Burr, "Barry Fairchild had a vulnerability that none of the others had, primarily because he has mental retardation."

Fairchild says, "To me it was a life or death situation. That's the way I saw it... They probably would've found my body in some ditch the next morning... I truly believe that."

In June, 1991, the district court upheld the conviction and death sentence of Barry Fairchild.

His attorneys have appealed to the Eighth Circuit Court of Appeals. Attorney Dick Burr, with a nod to the history of Little Rock, Arkansas, wonders whether justice can prevail. "This case is a question about whether black people who have been terrorized and who speak about it with humiliation, with emotion, with tears--whether those people can be believed when the likes of Tommy Robinson say, 'No, they're liars.'"

A Federal judge in August 1995 found that Fairchild had not fired the shots that killed Majorie Mason but Arkansas law allows the execution of accomplices to murder. No second suspect has ever been charged.

Barry Fairchild was executed by lethal injection in Arkansas on August 31st, 1995.

Sheriff Tommy Robinson became a U.S. Congressman from 1985 -1991 and ran for Congress as a Republican Party candidate in 2002.

Two former Pulaski County Sheriff Deputies, Frank Gibson and Calvin Rollins have admitted that physical assault and abuse were common interrogation tactics at the time of Barry Fairchild's arrest.

MARK EDWARD GARDNER

Born 1956 – executed by lethal injection in Arkansas on September 8th, 1999.

Shortly after 2:00 p.m. on December 12th, 1985, the bodies of Mr. and Mrs. Joyce and Sara McCurdy were discovered in the Joyce residence in Fort Smith, Arkansas. Mr. Joyce was found in one room tied to a chair by his own neckties. His feet had been bound and he had been gagged. A necktie was wrapped about his neck so tightly that it had to be cut free. Mrs. Joyce was found bound and gagged in one of the bedrooms. At the later case trial, the medical examiner testified that Mr. and Mrs. Joyce died of strangulation. Sara McCurdy was found in another bedroom with a belt wrapped around her neck. She too had been bound and gagged. Additionally, a coat hanger had been twisted about her neck. She was taken to a local hospital with the expectation that she might survive but was pronounced dead on arrival. The cause of death was strangulation. At trial, the State produced evidence that Sara McCurdy had also been raped.

Cindy Griggs, Sara McCurdy's sister and co-worker, testified later that an inventory of the items in her parents' home revealed that a bag of silver coins, money, knives, a purse, binoculars, and numerous pieces of jewellery were missing. She described the knives, purse, binoculars, and jewellery very distinctly.

Additional testimony by other witnesses established that Sara McCurdy had left work at 11:15 a.m. on December 12th to drop off her car, a 1977 Buick LaSabre, at her parents' home. It had been planned that Mr. Joyce would take Sara back to work after lunch, but she never returned. Calls to the Joyce residence between 12:30 and 2:00 went unanswered. Subsequently, the victims' bodies were discovered by a relative. It was determined at that time that Sara McCurdy's car was missing.

Earlier on December 12th, at approximately 3:30 a.m., Mark Gardner had checked into the Regal 8 Inn in Fort Smith. Gardner was already the subject of an arrest warrant issued in Illinois for armed robbery and out on parole after yet another armed robbery conviction. Shortly before 11:00 a.m. later that day he was seen walking in the direction of May Avenue in Fort Smith. Between 11:00 and 11:30, at a shop on May Avenue, Gardner asked for directions to Linwood Street. The directions given would have taken him within one block of the Joyce residence. The next time Gardner was seen was shortly before 2:00 p.m. near Pocola, Oklahoma. He was driving a 1977 Buick LaSabre later found abandoned near Pocola and identified as belonging to Sara McCurdy.

The abandoned vehicle had been left near a service station where Gardner took a bus to the Fort Smith bus station. He was described as carrying a purse matching the description of the one taken from the Joyce residence. From Fort Smith, Gardner took another bus to Little Rock. At the Little Rock bus station, he attempted to sell numerous pieces of jewellery and several silver coins to persons waiting in bus queues who later testified for the State at trial and described the jewellery and coins in detail. After his arrival in Little Rock, Gardner checked into the Downtowner Motor Inn and on December 13th he pawned some of the jewellery at Maxie's Pawn Shop in Little Rock.

Based on a description of Gardner and information that he was trying to pawn jewellery in Little Rock and obtain a ride to Fort Smith, undercover Arkansas State Police officers went to the Little Rock bus station in an unmarked vehicle and offered Gardner a ride to Fort Smith if he would pay for the gas. Gardner agreed. He was arrested on route to Fort Smith at a point near Clarksville. On that same day, officers obtained custody of the jewellery that had been pawned at Maxie's in Little Rock. That jewellery was taken to Clarksville where it was identified by Cindy Griggs as the jewellery missing from her parents' home.

On December 14th, the police searched Gardner's room at the Downtowner Motor Inn in Little Rock with a warrant. The search produced several items later identified as having been taken from the Joyce residence. On December 16th, one of the officers returned to the Downtowner Inn and took custody of certain items seen but not seized during the original search. These items had been removed and secured by employees of the Inn. Among those items was the purse Gardner had been carrying near Pocola which had belonged to Mrs. Joyce.

Gardner was convicted of first degree murder and given the death sentence. He was 29 at the time of the murders and just past 43 when his appeals ran out and he was executed on September 8th, 1999.

ANDREW DOUGLAS GOLDEN

Born May 25th, 1986 – died in a car crash July 2019.

The Westside Middle School massacre was a school shooting that occurred on March 24th, 1998 in Westside Middle School in Craighead County, Arkansas, United States, near Jonesboro. A total of five people, four female students and a teacher, were killed. Ten people, nine students and one teacher, were injured.

Scott Johnson, born August 11th, 1984 and Andrew Douglas Golden, born May 25, 1986 were middle school students who committed the massacre,

Mitchell Scott Johnson, 13 years old at the time of the attack, lived in Jonesboro with his mother, stepfather, and his brother. His parents divorced when he was seven, and his mother remarried to Terry Woodward, an inmate at the prison where she was a guard.

Johnson had a good relationship with his stepfather, and adults who remember him described him as being quiet and respectful. However, his fellow students at Westside Middle School described him as being a bully, who talked of wanting to belong to street gangs and smoke marijuana. He also spoke of "having a lot of killing to do" and holding a bitter grudge against Shannon Wright, his English teacher. His classmates also commented that he had a fascination with firearms.

Following the shooting, Johnson's attorney claimed that he had been sexually abused when he was 6 and 7 years old by a "family member of the day care where he was placed." One year prior to the shooting, 12-year-old Mitchell was charged with molesting a 3-year-old girl while visiting

Minnesota with his family. However, the record of the case was deleted because of Mitchell's age.

Andrew Douglas Golden lived in the Jonesboro area with his parents. By all accounts, he came from a stable and loving household, having a good relationship with both his parents. He was raised to be familiar with guns and their use at an early age; he was given his first firearm by his father when he was six years old. Golden's schoolmates also described him as a bully, and instigator of troublesome behaviour. He would often engage fist fights with other students, and would use profane language. A classmate once accused him of killing her cat with a BB gun.

On the night of March 23rd, 1998 Golden helped Johnson load his mother's 1991 Dodge Caravan with weapons, snack foods, and camping supplies.

The next day, Johnson stole his mother's keys and drove to the school with Golden. Johnson and parked the van in the middle of the woods outside of the backyard of the school, planning to return there once the massacre was over. Johnson sat on a hill in the backyard of the school while Golden went inside and pulled the fire alarm. Golden ran back and rejoined him on the hill with his weapon. As the students and teachers filed out of the building, thinking it was a routine fire drill, Johnson and Golden opened fire on them.

After they fired for four minutes, four students and a teacher were dead, and ten more were wounded. As the police arrived on the scene, Johnson and Golden ran into the woods back to the van. However, they failed to outrun the officers that were pursuing them, and were both arrested.

Due to their age, they were tried as juveniles, and were found guilty of 5 counts of murder. Following their convictions, Johnson and Golden were taken by National

Guard helicopter to Alexander, Arkansas, the location of the Youth Services Division's juvenile facility and the state's most secure juvenile facility.

Johnson was released on August 11th, 2005, on his 21st birthday. Originally he was to only be held until he turned 18 years old but added crimes added 3 years to his sentence.. He spent less than 2 years in jail for each murder that he committed. On release he was allowed to buy and own firearms.

Golden was released on May 25th, 2007, also his 21st birthday. Golden's exact whereabouts were then unknown until he applied for a concealed weapon permit in Arkansas on October 7th, 2008, under the name he now uses, Drew Douglas Grant. His application was denied by Arkansas state police, who noted that Golden had lied on the application about his previous residences and claimed it would be illegal for Golden to own or possess a firearm, though the reason for this is unclear. The assumed name that Golden was using had been unknown up until this point due to a gag order, but police were able to tie Andrew Golden to Grant through fingerprint records during the background check for the permit

On January 1st, 2007, Johnson was arrested after a traffic stop in Fayetteville, Arkansas on charges of carrying a weapon — a loaded 9 mm pistol — and possession of 21.2 grams of marijuana. Though the van Johnson was riding in was registered to him, the driver was 22-year-old Justin Trammell. Trammell and Johnson reportedly met at Alexander Youth Services Correctional Facility in Alexander, Arkansas, where Trammell was incarcerated after pleading guilty to the 1999 crossbow murder of his father, a crime committed when Trammell was just 15. The pair were roommates and provided officers with the same Fayetteville address. Trammel was cited for careless driving and released. Johnson was arrested for possession of marijuana and a loaded weapon and later released on a $1,000 bond. He had a court appearance on January 26th, 2007 at the Washington County, Arkansas courthouse.

Johnson was indicted by a federal grand jury on October 24th, 2007 for possession of a firearm while either using or addicted to a controlled substance. The U.S. Attorney's Office for the Western District of Arkansas reported that Johnson pleaded not guilty and was released on a $5,000 bond. Johnson's trial began on January 28th, 2008. After two days of testimony from the prosecution and the defence witnesses, Johnson was found guilty on a charge of possessing a weapon while being a drug user.

In February 2008, just days after his conviction, Johnson was arrested again, this time for possession of marijuana at the convenience store he worked at and on suspicion of using a stolen credit card.

On September 2008, US District court sentenced Mitchell Johnson to four years in prison on the weapon and drug charges. In his sentencing, the Judge expressed dismay that Johnson had not taken advantage of the chance he had to go straight. He told him "No matter your sentence, you still have a life, those killed in 1998 do not". On October 7th, 2008, Johnson pleaded guilty to a felony theft charge and misdemeanour possession of marijuana. He admitted that he stole a debit card left by a disabled man at the Bentonville gas station where he worked and subsequently used it to purchase a meal at a local Burger King. He also admitted that, at the time he was arrested, he was in possession of marijuana.

On November 14th, 2008, Johnson, now 24 years old, was sentenced to 12 years in prison for the theft charge and misdemeanour possession charges. Although Johnson could have faced up to 30 years, the sentence of 12 years was chosen because Johnson technically had no criminal record from the Jonesboro shooting.

On January 23rd, 2009, Johnson was sentenced to six additional years in prison for an additional charge of theft by receiving and financial identity fraud for using the stolen card to purchase a meal from a local Burger King. Circuit Judge William Storey told Johnson "You continue to run afoul of the law. I am hopeful this is the last time." This brought Johnson's combined state sentences to 18 years. He will be in his 30s before release.

On July 27th, 2019 Golden, then 33, was killed in a head-on car crash south of Cave City, Arkansas on Highway 167. It is thought that Stephanie Grant and a two year old child in the car who survived were his wife and child. As stated previously Golden changed his name to Drew Grant after the Westside Massacre.

JACK GORDON GREENE

Born March 13th, 1955 – sentenced to death in Arkansas on October 15th, 1992.

Around the 20th July 1991 Jack Greene killed his own brother Tommy in North Carolina by shooting him five times. He then stole his brother's car and left for Arkansas where he broke into the home of 69 year old Sidney Burnett and his wife on the 23rd July.

Mr. Burnett and his wife had previously befriended Mr. Greene and his wife when the Greenes sought help from them through a church charity program. The Burnetts gave the Greenes employment and a place to live. The Greenes apparently had marital difficulties. Mrs. Greene left Jack and soon after he returned to Johnson County briefly and went to the Burnett's. Mr. Greene apparently thought Mrs. Burnett had interfered in his relationship with his wife and responsible for his wife leaving him.

Sydney Burnett, a 69 year old preacher was home and Greene beat him, tied him up and shot him to death with the same gun that he had murdered his brother with.

Mr. Burnett's body was found in his home with his feet and hands bound. He had been shot in the chest and head and beaten with a hard object. He had been stabbed more than once, and his face had been mutilated. The State Medical Examiner testified that Mr. Burnett had been subjected to painful stabbing and beating while still alive. A .25-calibre firearm caused the bullet wounds.

After Mr. Burnett's body was discovered, Mr. Greene became a suspect, and he was arrested in Oklahoma while in possession of a .25-calibre pistol and ammunition. Upon his arrest as a person wanted in connection with Mr. Burnett's death, Mr. Greene told the arresting officer, "I'm your man," and he remarked that Mrs. Burnett had caused his wife to leave him and had wrongfully accused him previously of burning a building belonging to the Burnetts.

Greene was convicted of the Burnett murder in 1992. The sentence was death but was overturned on appeal. Twice more he was convicted and the conviction overturned. He also received a life sentence in North Carolina for the killing of his brother. In 2021 he seems to have exhausted his appeals and is waiting for an execution date.

JAMES WAYBERN HALL

Born January 28th, 1921 – executed by electrocution in Arkansas January 4th, 1946.

    James Hall married 19-year-old Fayrene Clemmons on March 14th, 1944 in Little Rock but their relationship was a stormy one, marked by a brief separation in June the same year.
    On September 28th, Hall paid a visit to his father-in-law, telling him that Fayrene had left him three days earlier. Police were notified by Hall that she was a missing person, logging reports that listed the young woman's known promiscuous behaviour. They closed their investigation after a week, declaring her a probable runaway. They thought this very likely the case when relatives received a Christmas card with Fayrene's signature, postmarked from Bakersfield, California. They really should have raised concerns when Jim Hall "borrowed" the card and envelope before officers had a chance to examine it, and it was subsequently "lost."
    On January 29th, 1945, loggers discovered an abandoned car in Ouachita County, southwest of Little Rock. There was a dead man slumped behind the wheel with a bullet in his heart. He was identified from fingerprints as Camden barber Carl Hamilton. The victim had been dead for several days when found, but homicide detectives had no reason to connect his murder with the disappearance of Fayrene Hall in Little Rock.
    The toll began to mount on February 1st, when E.C. Adams vanished en route to his job at a Little Rock war plant. His car was found outside of Fordyce, northwest of Camden in Dallas County, and his body later found in some

nearby scrub with a single bullet in his head. That same day, trucker Doyle Mulherin was reported as being long overdue on a scheduled meat delivery, his vehicle was found hours later near Stuttgart, 40-odd miles to the southeast of Little Rock, in Arkansas County. A search of the area turned up his body with a bullet in his head and his pockets emptied of $125 in company cash he was carrying.

Police were still without a suspect on March 2nd when James Hall was arrested in a Little Rock bar fight and fined $106.90 on his plea of guilty to simple assault. Authorities became more interested in Hall when an acquaintance told of loaning Hall a car on January 28th. There was a loaded pistol in the glove compartment, and a single round was missing from the clip when Hall returned the car on January 29th. Ballistics tests revealed the gun had been the one that shot and killed Carl Hamilton.

On March 9th, 1945, a burned-out car was found near Heber Springs, in Cleburne County. An incinerated body was recovered from the back seat and identified from dental charts as J.D. Newcomb, Jr., late of Little Rock.

A search of Jim Hall's lodgings meanwhile had revealed substantial quantities of ammunition and shaving gear stolen from Carl Hamilton. When picked up near Little Rock on March 15th, Hall confessed to the series of holdup-murders that had earned him less than $300 overall. He finally admitted Fayrene's murder and led detectives to where his wife was buried, they were surprised to learn a farmer had retrieved the skull months earlier. Identified from her crooked teeth, Fayrene was finally laid to rest.

Convicted of murder after a two-day trial, in May 1945, Hall was sentenced to death. He was executed by electrocution January 4th, 1946.

WILBURN A. HENDERSON

Born 1942 - executed by lethal injection in Arkansas on July 8th, 1998.

Wilburn Henderson was convicted of the capital murder of Willa Dean O'Neal on February 2nd, 1982, and was sentenced to death.

His first trial was declared a mistrial when several jurors admitted they had seen the extensive media publicity about the case. At the second trial, the prosecution presented evidence showing that Willa Dean O'Neal was found shot to death behind the counter of the second hand furniture store she owned and operated with her husband.

The police established she was murdered between 1:40 p.m., when her husband Bob O'Neal, daughter Glenda Fleetwood, and son-in-law Ricky Fleetwood last saw her, and approximately 2:00 p.m., when a mail man and several customers discovered the body. The cash register was found open and at least $41 was missing.

A key piece of evidence implicating Wilburn Henderson was a folded sheet of yellow paper found on the floor of the furniture store. The victim's daughter testified she had not seen the paper there earlier in the day. On the paper were two telephone numbers, the name of a real estate agent, and a description of a lake cabin. Police contacted the real estate agent who stated Henderson had made an appointment to discuss buying the lake cabin described on the sheet of paper. Henderson did not keep that appointment. This piece of paper was the sole physical evidence connecting Henderson with the scene of the murder.

Henderson, aware that he was a suspect, fled to Houston where he was arrested by Houston police. Police by then had discovered that Henderson had taken a .22 calibre pistol out of pawn a few days before the murder, and had returned it after the murder. Ballistics evidence at his later trial indicated O'Neal was killed by a .22 calibre pistol, but could not conclusively match the bullet to Henderson's gun.

Arkansas police travelled to Houston to question Henderson who confessed he was at the murder scene and claimed he had seen a man called Ollie Brown kill O'Neal. Henderson later recanted the confession and stated he confessed only because he feared the police would harm him.

At trial, Henderson testified that he was in Springdale, Arkansas, at 12:00 noon on the day of the murder and could not possibly have driven to the murder site in Fort Smith in time to commit the murder. His alibi was corroborated by Selena Henderson, his wife at the time, who claimed to have been with him in Springdale on that day. Henderson explained that he must have dropped the yellow sheet of paper when he was shopping in the O'Neals' store a few days before the murder.

Based on this evidence only the jury found Henderson guilty of the murder. At the penalty phase, Henderson's mother testified that he was a loving son, and another witness testified that he had been doing good Christian work while in jail. Defence counsel presented no other mitigating evidence. The jury sentenced him to death.

Henderson, 56, was executed by injection on July 8th, 1998. "I am an innocent man," he told the warden. "God forgive you for what you do."

An interesting aside...

Immediately after the murder, Willa Dean O'Neal's daughter and a stepdaughter, both children from previous marriages, told police that they suspected Bob O'Neal.

The daughters said in interviews with the press that O'Neal had abused their mother and that she had begun to talk about divorcing him. Willa Dean O'Neal had also filed an alienation of affection suit against a woman who was having an affair with her husband.

"My first instinct was that it was Bob," stepdaughter Glenda Palmer said. "He was verbally abusive, mentally abusive—just a mean man."

According to court records and interviews, Bob O'Neal, on the day before the murder, asked Willa Dean O'Neal's daughter, Glenda Fleetwood, where her mother wanted to be buried. And on the morning of the murder, he asked Fleetwood to break from the family's usual routine and work with him on a house clearance instead of at the store with her mother.

That afternoon Bob O'Neal, Fleetwood and her husband stopped by the store where her mother was alone inside working before they went to salvage materials from the clearance house. Before they left, O'Neal went back inside briefly. He told Fleetwood and her husband to wait outside, according to interviews and court records. After he came back out, they left for the work site.

A few minutes later, O'Neal sent Fleetwood back to get a root beer from the store. When she returned with a soda and mentioned she had bought it at another store, he became angry and insisted she return to the family business for electrical tape, according to court records and interviews.

That was when she discovered her mother's body. Fleetwood summoned police and, accompanied by an officer, went to tell O'Neal his wife was dead.

"When I came up with the police, he said, 'Somebody killed her, didn't they?" Fleetwood told the press.

That comment bothered Ron Fields, the former prosecuting attorney who twice tried Henderson. "The troubling thing," Fields said, "was him having this psychic statement—you know, knowing she was already dead. O'Neal couldn't ever explain it."

STEVEN DOUGLAS HILL

Born 1966 – executed by lethal injection in Arkansas May7th, 1992.

On October 15th, 1984, Steven Hill, 18, and Michael Cox escaped from an outside work unit of the Arkansas Department of Correction. Shortly after dark the same day, they arrived at the home of an elderly couple, Merle and Billie Jo Rice.

They robbed the Rices of money, a 16-gauge shotgun, an automatic carbine, and a 20-gauge automatic shotgun, and tied them up. Hill threatened to rape Mrs. Rice and told Mr. Rice he was going to kill him but Cox dissuaded Hill from both actions.

The pair left the Rice home at approximately 10:30 p.m. in the Rice's pickup truck and proceeded to an unoccupied residence some two miles from the Rice home. Alerted by Mr Rice Several police officers soon arrived at the scene after spotting the Rice's pickup parked in the driveway.

As officer Robert Klein and Lieutenant Conrad Patillo approached the garage behind which Hill was hiding, Klein was shot and killed by a 20-gauge shotgun blast. Patillo was fired upon but not injured. Several hours later, at approximately 4:30 a.m., tear gas forced Hill and Cox, who had barricaded themselves in the garage, to surrender.

The evidence at trial indicated that Cox had hidden himself in the attic of the garage prior to Klein's murder, and did not see or participate in the shooting. After his surrender, Cox was found in the attic with an automatic carbine that had not been fired.

The 20-gauge automatic shotgun, the murder weapon, and twenty-one shotgun shells were found in a corner of the lower garage room where Hill had hidden himself behind a mattress. Hill and Cox were taken to police headquarters where they were read their rights and made videotape statements. Hill admitted using the 20-gauge shotgun to kill Klein.

Steven Hill was charged with capital murder, attempted capital murder, escape, burglary, theft, aggravated robbery, and kidnapping. He pleaded guilty to all charges except capital murder and attempted capital murder. Hill was tried by a jury and found guilty of both the capital murder and attempted capital murder charges. After Hill and Cox were tried separately, the jury imposed the death sentence on Hill for the capital murder charge and fifty years imprisonment on the attempted capital murder charge. Cox was sentenced to 86 years in prison.

At the exhausting of his appeals Hill was denied clemency by Arkansas Governor Bill Clinton and the United States Supreme Court. Steven Hill was executed by lethal injection on May7th, 1992.

JAMES WILLIAM HOLMES

Born 1957 – executed by lethal injection August 3rd, 1994.

See under HOYT FRANKLIN CLINES

DAVID DEWAYNE JOHNSON

Born January 10th, 1963 – executed by lethal injection in Arkansas December 19th, 2000.

The victim in this case, Leon Brown, a sixty-seven-year-old male, first went to work for Little Rock Crate and Basket Company in 1967, he worked there for a few years, left, returned in 1982, and continued to work there until he was murdered. During the last few years he worked as a night watchman only on Friday and Saturday nights.

On the evening of Saturday, September 2nd, 1989, while on duty, he wore a black leather John Brown type of police belt and holster to carry his .41 calibre Smith and Wesson pistol, and four empty shell casings.

He was known to carry the empty casings, although no one knew the reason. He also carried a watchman's clock, which is a device that looks something like an old-fashioned leather covered circular style canteen with a paper disc on the outside.

As he made his rounds, he would stop at designated locations which had permanent station keys and insert one of the keys in his watchman's clock. It would punch a hole in the paper disc. That hole would reflect the time that he had stopped at that particular station.

Little Rock Crate and Basket Company was located at 1623 East Fourteenth Street, which is at the end of Fourteenth Street in Little Rock.

It manufactured fruit and vegetable containers, baskets, and wire bound crates. It consisted of warehouses on both sides of the street, a log yard, and an office which is located at the end of one of the warehouses.

The office area, comprised of five offices, built of concrete blocks and had three steel doors which were locked with dead bolt locks. It had windows which opened into a lunchroom which was located at the end of the warehouses. The warehouses were built of corrugated steel, and on September afternoons, it got hot inside them, so it was not unusual for the workers to open the warehouse doors to cool the building.

The doors were open at 6:30pm on the evening of September 2nd, 1989. The workers would not have worried about security because Fourteenth Street at that location was a private street, owned by Little Rock Crate and Basket, with no through traffic, and the business was surrounded by a high chain link fence with barbed wire on top.

Leon Brown had a number of long standing friends who worked at Little Rock Crate and Basket Company, and he enjoyed going to work a little early so he could chat with them. His night watchman's shift began at 4 p.m. He went in early on the 2nd and talked with his friends and then, at work time, began his rounds.

Dudley Swann, the principal shareholder in Little Rock Crate and Basket, received a call from a customer at about 4:30pm that afternoon. The customer wanted some crates delivered immediately, and Swann had to find truck drivers who were willing to work on the Labor Day weekend. He was at his home when he received the customer's call and did not have the drivers' telephone numbers there, so he went to the works to get them.

As he drove up to the company office area at about 6:30pm, he saw a white Delta 88 Oldsmobile automobile stuck in the drainage ditch beside the private street. The driver was trying to drive it out of the ditch but having no luck and the wheels were just spinning..

Swann parked his car, walked over to the white Oldsmobile, and asked the driver to leave it and come back the next day to get his car because he did not want the driver on the premises after dark. Swann later identified David Johnson as the driver of the white Oldsmobile.

Swann went into the building offices and there saw Leon Brown on duty. He told Brown about the white Oldsmobile and stated that he had asked the driver to leave and come back the next day to retrieve his car.

Swann went into his office and, over about a fifteen-minute period making phone calls he got his deliveries sorted with drivers. He left the office area and went into the lunchroom area and again saw Brown. He asked Brown if the driver had left, and Brown motioned toward a pay telephone located on the wall. Swann looked there and saw Johnson using it. He went over to him and said, "I thought I asked you to walk on out." Johnson replied, "Yes sir, I am in just a moment. I need to make one or two telephone calls to try to find some friends but they're all at work." Brown told Swann, "Don't worry about anything. Everything's all right." Swann made a note of the license plate number on the white Oldsmobile and left at 6:50 p.m.

The next morning, Sunday, the 3rd, at 7:15, George Wood, another part-time watchman, came to the warehouses to check on Brown, as he usually did when Brown had done a night shift. He stood outside and called out for Leon Brown.

There was no response and he waited ten or fifteen minutes for Brown to complete one of his rounds, but Brown did not appear.

By then, Lawrence Sloan had come to work the day watch, and after about fifteen minutes more, the two of them decided to go into the building. The gate was locked, but they went around to one of the doors that had been left open to cool the building the evening before. Just inside, in the lunchroom area, where Swann had last seen the Johnson and Brown, they saw Brown's body lying face-down in a large pool of blood. He had been bludgeoned to death with a piece of 2" x 4" wood that was found nearby.

Three of the blows to his head were made with such force that his skull was crushed, part of it was dislodged and rammed into his brain, and his brain was also crushed.

The medical examiner later estimated that the blows to the head were so forceful that 300 to 400 pounds of pressure per square inch had been inflicted on his skull.

An image of the extent of the damage to the victim's skull is created by the fact that upon arriving at the scene experienced detectives thought the victim had been shot in the head. His false teeth were found six feet away from his head, and his glasses were found alongside.

The vending machines in the lunchroom area had been turned over and broken into. The windows into the office area had been forced open and the offices had been entered. Papers had been strewn about, desk drawers had been opened, and the pay telephone had been torn off the wall.

Among the missing items were a typewriter, a Sharp brand calculator, two cameras, tools, three pistols, a fountain pen, a briefcase, a television set, three Motorola brand handheld radios, and a battery charger.

The police were called; they quickly responded and immediately began their investigation. Officer Todd Vint was assigned to watch the white Delta 88 Oldsmobile automobile that was still stuck in the ditch outside.

At about 11 o'clock that morning, a blue and white pickup stopped beside the white Oldsmobile, and three people got out and began to try to get it out of the ditch. The three were Terrie Dickerson; her father, Elmer Richardson; and the Johnson. Dudley Swann saw them and told officer Vint that Johnson was the man he had seen the evening before, first trying to get the car out of the ditch and then later inside the building.

Police work developed many additional facts pointing at Johnson as the killer which were subsequently proven at trial. Steve Rowell told the police he was the manager of Lucky's Seafood in Little Rock and that Johnson worked there and was supposed to report for work at either 4:00 or 5:00 p.m. on the 2nd but did not do so.

At a few minutes after 7:00 p.m. on the 2nd, Johnson had called Rowell and told him that he could not come to work because he was in jail. In fact, he was not in jail, and at that time, the police were not looking for him. Robert Sanders told the police that he saw a low-slung black car parked in front of Little Rock Crate and Basket Company a little after 9:00pm on the night of the 2nd.

Terrie Dickerson told the police that, at about 11:00am on the morning of the 2nd, before the murder, Johnson came to her house and told her that his car was out of gasoline and asked to borrow her car. She stated that he owned a low-slung black Oldsmobile Cutlass automobile. She loaned him her white Oldsmobile Delta 88. He left in her car, came back about 2:30pm that afternoon, and left again in her car at about 2:45pm.

She did not see him again until about 9:00pm that night, the 2nd, when he returned on foot and told her that the police had been chasing him and that he had gotten her car stuck in a ditch.

In fact, the police were not chasing him. He left her house on foot, but later came back in his low-slung black car, and brought into her house three Motorola brand handheld radios and a Sharp brand calculator. Later, she went with him when he drove his black car to a friend, Priscilla Marshall's house. At that time she saw some guns and tools in his car. He took the guns and tools into Priscilla's house.

The next morning, September 3rd, Terrie and Johnson went to the home of Terrie's father, Elmer Richardson. They asked him to drive them to the Little Rock Crate and Basket Company so they could get Terrie's white Oldsmobile out of the ditch.

As they drove up in his pickup truck, they were spotted by Officer Vint and Johnson was seen by Dudley Swann and was arrested by the police. Subsequently, the radios and calculator were recovered from Terrie's house. They were identified as part of the property taken from the Little Rock Crate and Basket Company.

Priscilla Marshall told the police that Johnson came to her house on the morning of the 3rd, told her that his girlfriend was moving to North Little Rock, and said he needed to store some guns and tools.

From her house the police later recovered the battery charger, a .38 calibre pistol, a Magnavox brand television set, cameras, tools, a fountain pen, and Leon Brown's .41 calibre Smith and Wesson revolver.

Each of the items was identified as property taken from Little Rock Crate and Basket. Connie Manuel testified that Johnson came to her house at about 10:00pm on the night of the 2nd, remained a few minutes, left, and came back between midnight and 1:00 a.m. on the 3rd. At that time, he washed his clothes and took a bath. He spent the rest of the night with her. Her mother, Luella Shavis, gave the washed clothes, including his tennis shoes, to the police.

The police found one of Johnson's palm prints on the coin box which had been ripped out of the soft drink vending machine in the lunchroom area, and removed one of his fingerprints from the inside of an office window. Both prints were positively identified as being Johnson's.

Johnson's tennis shoes, which had been recovered from Luella Shavis, had human blood on them, but it was not in sufficient quantity to identify the type.

Hair samples found on the 2" x 4" wood were compatible with the hair of Leon Brown. The paper disc from the watchman's clock reflected that Leon Brown did not make his round through the building at 7:00 p.m. on September 2nd.

On legal advice Johnson did not testify at trial. One defence witness, Ella Mae Richardson, testified at the guilt phase of the trial that the Johnson phoned her at 5:00 or 5:30 p.m. on the 2nd, and another witness, public defender Llewellyn J. Marczuk, testified that detective Mark Stafford told him that Johnson might not have committed the crime alone.

The detective denied making the statement. The other defence witness took the Fifth Amendment.

After hearing the above testimony, the jury unanimously found Johnson guilty of capital murder. The punishment phase of the trial was then held, and the jury found one aggravating circumstance, that the murder was committed for pecuniary gain, and one mitigating circumstance, that the appellant was a model prisoner and could conform to prison life and be a productive member of the prison society.

The jury weighed the two and unanimously determined beyond a reasonable doubt that the aggravating circumstance outweighed the mitigating circumstance and determined that appellant should be sentenced to death by lethal injection. David Johnson was executed on December 19th, 2000.

MITCHELL SCOTT JOHNSON

Responsible for the Westside Middle School shootings with Andrew Golden

Born August 11th, 1984 – sentenced to imprisonment until age 21. Released on August 11th, 2005 after 7 years 4 months.

See under ANDREW GOLDEN

STACEY EUGENE JOHNSON

Born November 26th, 1969 – sentenced to death September 23rd, 1994.

Carol Heath was brutally murdered in her duplex apartment in DeQueen on either the night of April 1st, 1993, or the early morning hours of April 2nd, 1993. She was beaten, strangled, and had her throat slit while her two young children, Ashley, age six, and Jonathan, age two, were home.

These facts regarding the murder and its aftermath are gleaned from the pre-trial and trial testimonies. At approximately 6:45 a.m. on April 2nd, 1993, Rose Cassidy, the victim's sister-in-law, knocked on Heath's door but did not receive an answer. Because the door was unlocked, she entered and found Carol Heath's partially nude body lying on the living room floor in a pool of blood. She ran across the street to call the police and then returned to check on her niece, Ashley, and nephew Jonathan, whom she saw looking out of the bedroom window. Cassidy testified that she asked

Ashley what had happened. Ashley responded, according to Cassidy: "Somebody had broke in", and I said "who?", and she said, "A black man." Carol Heath was white.

Sergeant Keith Tucker of the DeQueen Police Department testified that he found Carol Heath's body naked except for a t-shirt that had been pushed up around her neck. He stated that her body was located between a couch which was tilted up onto its back legs and a coffee table which had apparently been moved toward the middle of the room. DeQueen Chief of Police James Smith arrived at the apartment later and testified that when he pulled the t-shirt away from the victim's neck, he saw that her throat had been slashed.

Dr. Frank Peretti, an associate medical examiner for the State Crime Laboratory, testified that Carol Heath's death was caused by cutting her neck, strangulation, and blunt-force head injuries. He stated that her attacker had left a four-inch by two-inch cut wound on her neck that went one-quarter inch into her spine. He observed that she had several bruises and abrasions on her head and face, that she had injuries on her hands and arms consistent with defensive wounds, that she had a bite mark on the nipple of her right breast and an abrasion on her left breast, and that there was a one-quarter-inch contusion on her right labia minora. Dr. Peretti could not conclude, based on the physical evidence, that she had been either sexually assaulted or raped.

Officer James Behling, a criminal investigator with the DeQueen Police Department, testified that he observed a pair of panties next to Carol Heath's right thigh. He noted an area of light-colour liquid between and around the legs and below the genital area of the victim. An empty douche bottle and an empty "Lifestyles" condom box were found in the bathroom sink.

On April 5th, 1993, Kenneth Bryan found a purse in the woods between DeQueen and Horatio which he later realized belonged to the victim. He took Officer Behling to the location. Officer Behling examined the area and found a bloody pullover green shirt, a bloody white t-shirt, and a bloody towel. Lisa Sakevicius, an expert with the State Crime Laboratory's trace evidence section, testified that hairs microscopically similar to Carol Heath's hair were found on all three of these items. She further testified that some other hairs retrieved from under the victim's left breast, from the floor beside the victim, and from the white t-shirt were of Negroid origin. Jane Parsons, a forensic serologist, testified for the State that no semen was found at the scene. She admitted that the finding of semen would be unlikely, if the perpetrator used a condom and douched the victim.

DNA evidence was introduced at trial. Melisa Weber, a staff molecular biologist at Cellmark Diagnostics, conducted a Restriction Fragment Length Polymorphism [RFLP] test on the green shirt for the State and testified that to a reasonable degree of scientific certainty the blood matched that of Carol Heath. She also conducted a Polymerase Chain Reaction [PCR] test on several items, including the white t-shirt found in the park, a cigarette butt found in the green shirt, and hairs taken from the body of Carol Heath and near to where the body was located. With respect to the white t-shirt, Weber testified that the victim could not be excluded as the source of the blood and that the probability of this DNA having come from another Caucasian was 1 in 12,000. With respect to the cigarette butt and hairs, Weber opined that Stacey Johnson could not be excluded and that the probability that another African-American was the donor of the DNA in question was 1 in 250.

Officer Hayes McWhirter, an investigator with the Arkansas State Police, talked with Carol Heath's daughter, six year old Ashley Heath, on the afternoon of April 2nd, 1993. Also present at the time was Cynthia Emerson, a supervisor with the Department of Human Services. Officer McWhirter made the following notes from that conversation and used these notes to refer to when he testified at the Johnson pre-trial hearings and at trial:

Ashley stated her mother and she were on the couch when someone knocked on the door. Ashley got up and opened the door. She confirmed that the picture No. 3, Stacey Johnson, is the person that came in the door. Ashley looked at six different pictures of black males. "Mother likes Branson. He works at In Your Ear. (Branson Ramsay was a black friend of Carol Heath) The black male asked where Branson was. The black male used a girl sounding name. He had on a black hat with something hanging down in the back. He had on a green shirt and sweater. When they were talking, the black male said he had just got out of jail. The black male was mad at mother for dating Branson. He had been over two other times, but it was a long time ago. I saw them fighting. Then I saw mother laying on the floor. I saw the black male leave and he got up and he got in a brown truck, I think. I saw a knife and a gun. The brown truck was parked beside the house. Mother looked out the window. When he knocked, then she let him in. While mother was laying on the floor, the black male walked into the bathroom. We were hiding in the closet. I came out the door to the bathroom and the black male had a knife in his hand beside mommy. She was on the floor bleeding. After he left, I went in and saw momma bleeding. Jonathan looked at mommy twice. She was covered in blood. We went to bed and then this morning when someone knocked on the door, I was scared to open the door. When Rose screamed, I knew she saw mommy with blood all over her. Every time I saw the black male, he had clothes on."

Officer McWhirter testified that he handed Ashley a stack of seven photographs, and she picked Johnson out of the photo line ups twice. Johnson was subsequently arrested in Albuquerque, New Mexico.

Johnson went to court indicted on first degree murder and sentenced to death. The appeal court named it a mistrial after Johnson's lawyers stated that Ashley was prevented from taking the witness stand as she was deemed incompetent so to do by the prosecution medical team. Her comments to Officer McWhirter were also not admitted. It also has transpired that DNA evidence was found on the clothes retrieved from the woods and at the crime scene which was not Johnson's. Nothing at the crime scene related back to Johnson. It also became knowledge that between the first and second trials Carol Heath's family schooled Ashley incase she was called to the witness stand telling her she must keep Johnson behind bars with her grandmother telling her he will kill Ashley if they let him out. The defence counsel was denied access to the notes and records made by the Southwest Arkansas Counselling and Mental Health Centre on the treatment of Ashley which split the appeal court judges as much of it referred to her admittance of the family pressure on her. A second mistrial was granted.

Further appeals followed and in June 2023 a federal appeals court ruled Johnson may sue the state of Arkansas to have new DNA tests run to clear him of Carol Heath's murder in 1993. He submits that DNA evidence may show Heath's boyfriend of the time, Branson Ramsay, to be the killer.

Johnson now 53, has spent over a quarter of a century on death row.

JACK HAROLD JONES

Born August 10th, 1964 –executed by lethal injection April 24th, 2017. His body exhumed 2018 and DNA taken that tied him to another murder.

Jack Harold Jones Jr. was an American serial killer who murdered at least three women in Florida and Arkansas between 1983 and 1995. Convicted of two murders during his lifetime and executed in 2017 he was posthumously linked via DNA to the third murder, for which another man had been imprisoned.

On May 2nd, 1983, Regina Harrison, a 20-year-old college student, left her parents' home for a nightly bike ride in Hollywood's's North Beach neighbourhood, but failed to return home. Friends and family found her nude body in the woods in West Lake Park. She had been strangled to death and her body discarded. During the subsequent investigation, witnesses reported that they had seen the woman riding accompanied by a skinny, long-haired man on a black bike.

There were no leads in the case for five months, until a detective from Fort Lauderdale, John Curcio, saw a programme about the case on TV. He had been a member of an investigative unit which had captured Ronald Henry Stewart, a serial rapist who had terrorized women in Broward County and Harrison County Mississippi, during the late 1980s, Curcio noticed that Stewart resembled the sketch of the suspect, in addition to being in possession of a black bike at the time of his arrest. A witness who said they had seen Regina and her alleged killer on the beach pointed to Ronald Stewart as the man she had seen, and he was soon charged with Harrison's murder. In order to avoid the death penalty,

Stewart entered a plea of no contest and was given 50 years imprisonment in January 1985, to run concurrently with his other sentences for the sexual offenses. Although several factors pointed towards his innocence in the case, including the fact that his fingerprints did not match those found at the crime scene, Stewart confessed to the crime. He never repudiated the confession nor claimed it was coerced while serving his time. Stewart died behind bars from cancer in 2008.

Lorraine "Lori" Anne Barrett, a 32-year-old tourist from Bridgeville, Pennsylvania was last seen at the Elbo Room, a bar located at the corner of Las Olas Boulevard and the A1A State road. According to witnesses, she was accompanied by a heavily tattooed man to her motel room at the Days Inn Lauderdale Surf Motel on Seabreeze Boulevard. At about noon on June 1st, 1991, her body was found by a cleaning lady. She had been raped and strangled.

Immediately following the body's discovery, police created a facial composite, complete with descriptions of the suspect's tattoos of barbed wire and hearts etched with names, and distributed it around Broward County. However, it didn't bring out any names and the case quickly went cold.

On June 6th, 1995, Mary Phillips and her 11-year-old daughter, Lacey, were attacked at her office in Bald knob, Arkansas. Jones, equipped with latex gloves, a wire, and a BB gun, broke into the office, raped and murdered Mary, and beat Lacey so brutally that she appeared to be dead. Jones tied the child to a chair in the bathroom and left.

The local sheriff's department dispatched three officers to the scene. Upon arrival, one officer entered the building and found Mary Phillips, deceased. He left the building and told the other officers that it was a scene of a homicide.

When they re-entered the building, they located Phillips' 11 year old daughter, Lacey, in the bathroom, tied to a chair, beaten severely about the head and covered in blood.

The officers initially believed Lacey to be dead due to the severity of her injuries. However, while taking flash photographs of the bathroom crime scene, Lacey turned her head and looked at the crime scene photographer. She was rushed to a nearby hospital for treatment. Once her condition stabilized, she gave a description of her assailant, a man with a tattoo on his arm and a teardrop tattoo under his left eye. The officers present during her interview identified the man she described as Jack Harold Jones, an Ohio native who was well known to the police. Jones was brought in for interrogation and confessed to the crime. He was brought to trial, found guilty, and sentenced to death for killing Mary Phillips.

While awaiting execution on Arkansas's Death Row, Jones's DNA was entered into CODIS, the nationwide DNA database. Years later, in 2003, it was matched to the DNA evidence of the Lori Barrett case. A second test was conducted at the state crime lab in Arkansas, which conclusively proved that Jack Jones was the perpetrator. The Florida authorities issued an extradition warrant for Jones, who by this time was appealing his death sentence in Arkansas for the third time. He was eventually tried for the Barrett murder, found guilty, sentenced to life imprisonment, and returned to await his execution back in Arkansas.

Over the years, Jones's execution was stayed several times, due to illnesses such as high blood pressure and diabetes, which resulted in one of his legs being amputated. According to his sister Lynn, Jones had suffered sexual and physical abuse as a child, which led to alcohol and drug dependency. Jones himself expressed regret over his actions and agreed with his sentence, explaining that he was haunted by the ghosts of his victims and was incapable of forgiving himself for what he had done.

On April 24th, 2017, Jones was executed at the Cummins Unit, Arkansas, along with fellow rapist-murderer Marcel Williams, marking the first double execution in the country in 17 years. Jones and Williams were two of four inmates executed in Arkansas in April 2017, the other two were convicted murderers Ledell Lee and Kenneth Williams Jones' last meal consisted of fried chicken, potato logs with tartar sauce, beef jerky bites, three candy bars, a chocolate milkshake, and fruit punch.

Shortly before his execution, he gave his sister a letter he had written in 2006, with instructions to open it a year after his execution date. In the letter, he confessed in detail to the murder of Regina Harrison, providing details only the killer would know. This revelation led to his body being exhumed and his DNA tested, and in February 2019, the Broward County Attorney's Office officially announced that Jones was the real killer, not Ronald Stewart. A spokeswoman for the attorney's office, Paula McMahon, said in a press release that they would work to vacate Stewart's conviction, and would further investigate Jones' past in order to determine if he had killed other victims in Florida, or elsewhere around the country.

GORDON WENDELL KAHL

Born January 8th, 1920 – killed in a shoot-out with police on June 3rd, 1984.

This is a pretty amazing story of FBI revenge.

In 1968, Tax Protestor Gordon Kahl stopped filing IRS 1040 Income Tax Returns. For 9 years the IRS ignored him, but in 1977 after he spoke on an evening radio talk show regarding the illicitness of the income tax system, over 250 phone calls would come into the radio station over the next two days supporting Kahl and pledging never to file another tax return. And with that, the IRS came down on Kahl like a ton of bricks. They quickly assembled a case against him and two weeks later threw a criminal prosecution against him for violating Title 26, Section 7203 "Willful Failure to File".

Gordon Kahl was a low-income farmer not even meeting minimal statutory standards for threshold income levels achieved before being required to file 1040s, but that was not about to stop the IRS, who are good at changing the facts by creating new facts.

Kahl was convicted and incarcerated. When out of the Leavenworth Federal Penitentiary on parole, Kahl left the Texas judicial district he was confined to by claiming that some aspect of the Restriction Order was defective. He moved to North Dakota -- and there, he met his fate. A criminal Summons issued from a Federal Court in Midland, Texas was served on Gordon Kahl on August 8th, 1980, charging him with a misdemeanour. Kahl responded by informing the Court that he would not be appearing, and the matter was allowed to be deferred until March 31st, 1982, when the Justice Department obtained a Federal Arrest Warrant citing his parole violation.

That Warrant was held up again until it was sent to the U.S. Marshals Office in Fargo, North Dakota on February 13th, 1983. The United States Marshals and the Federal Court in Texas knew of his whereabouts in North Dakota at all times.

Once again Gordon Kahl had attracted the attention of the United States Government. With Ronald Reagan acquiescing indifferently as President, and with William French Smith sitting as Attorney General, the word came down the pipeline to GET RID OF GORDON KAHL, and the stage was set for the kind of confrontation the Feds wanted.

A violent attack was planned against Gordon Kahl at his farmhouse, and it was going to be well publicized. The attack would be in the form of a roadblock, it would be in the evening hours, and it would occur in a remote rural area. The timing of the attack in February of 1983 was selected to coincide with the trials of other related criminal prosecutions then going on that would be favourably tipped towards the Government, as the juries were exposed to what would be surfacing visibly on the news as the Gordon Kahl "incident."

From his farm in Heaton, North Dakota, both Gordon Kahl, along with his neighbours, and the Chief of Police of Medina, North Dakota, Darrell Graff, had received several advanced notices that the United States Marshals were planning a very unpleasant reception for Gordon Kahl, and in the case of Darrell Graff, he was told bluntly to stay out of it.

Rather than meet his adversaries face-to-face to settle the grievance at that lower level, Gordon Kahl ignored the gathering storm and tossed aside the Warrant, thus giving his adversaries the benefit of intensifying the impending confrontation into an elevated level -- a level that originates out of the barrel of a gun, where the Feds were quite likely to prevail.

On the 14th of February, 1983, Gordon Kahl, accompanied by his wife and son Yori, left a meeting in a Medina, North Dakota commercial district and headed home. Gordon Kahl was under surveillance and he knew it. He could have been picked up at the meeting, but the Feds had a surprise for him and wanted the remoteness of a rural environment. His son Yori detected something dangerous in the air, and so he took his father's jacket and cap and wore those himself on the ride home that afternoon.

Not far from his farmhouse a roadblock had been set up by U.S. Marshal Kenneth Muir. It was a very unusual roadblock in that it had an ambulance and firetruck in attendance. The Marshal had not come to arrest, but to murder. Bringing neither the Arrest Warrant, nor any identification, Deputy Muir brought his gun and had orders to terminate Gordon Kahl.

Arriving at the roadblock, Gordon's son, Yori Kahl, fled the pickup truck and ran to a nearby telephone pole for cover. Thinking that Yori was his dad Gordon, Marshal Muir opened the shooting by firing several shots at Yori.

Yori did not fall to the ground quick enough to satisfy the killer Marshal, so Marshal Muir kept on shooting until Yori fell. Later, after spending a while at the hospital, Yori Kahl would actually survive to be charged with murder, and later convicted by a jury in a Star Chamber that was highly pressured by the U.S. Marshals and had numerous other fatal irregularities that would never survive reversal on appeal.

Back at the evening roadblock, after seeing his own son cut down by Marshal Muir, Gordon Kahl grabbed a gun and let Marshal Muir have it, killing him and Deputy Marshal Robert Cheshire. Injured was Deputy Marshal James Hopson. Staying in the background, looking at all of this shooting was Chief Darrell Graff of the Medina Police Department, who was told in that he was to stay out of it.

Gordon Kahl went over to the telephone pole in the darkness, dragged his son Yori, white with blood loss and bleeding profusely, over to an unmarked police car, drove him to a hospital back in Medina, and then as a thick fog quickly settled in on the Fargo countryside, Gordon Kahl sped away into the night.

Soon, a swarm of military storm troopers descended on Fargo, in military clothing and using military trucks. They were on search and destroy orders. Gordon Kahl was immediately placed on the FBI's ten most wanted list, and was the subject of the most intensive fugitive search in the history of the FBI. It was a massive operation.

A tight clampdown was put out in North Dakota, accompanied with extensive random stops of motor vehicles, but nothing ever turned up. For Gordon Kahl, thousands of armed forces were called into search the surrounding North Dakota countryside. Every available private bounty hunter known to the FBI was hired and put on the case, but fugitive Gordon Kahl slipped through it all.

For the next three months, Kahl had found a home with some friends, Mr. and Mrs. Ginter, and a Mr. Art Russell, who kept moving him quietly from house to house. It was rather obvious to anyone that if he was ever found, he would be killed immediately.

In time, Mr. Russell's daughter, Karen Russell Robertson, noticed that her father was hiding Gordon Kahl and she went to the FBI and told them. She was given $25,000 and the promise of immunity from prosecution.

The rural house where Gordon Kahl was staying was placed under FBI surveillance; but the results were inconclusive. On the morning of June 4th, a special FBI team and the FBI SWAT TEAM, left their home base in Washington, D.C. and flew into Lawrence County, Arkansas on a private FBI jet. There, they were met by local FBI agents, other FBI agents, the Arkansas State Police, the Sheriff of Lawrence County, Arkansas, his deputies, and a confluence of United States Marshals assembled from across the country.

Later in the afternoon, it all began. The quiet, isolated and remote house was cordoned off, roadblocks were set up, and all without Gordon Kahl detecting anything amiss. Soon that afternoon, Mr. Ginter left the house alone and he was stopped down the road. He claimed his wife, Norma Ginter, was in the house alone and Sheriff Gene Matthews went to the front door to remove Mrs. Ginter from the scene.

With her out of the way, the FBI started shooting and saturated the house with bullets; but the earth shelter house was made with concrete walls and Gordon Kahl survived through it all without a scratch. 36 year old local Sheriff, Gene Matthews, was killed by friendly.

After a while, as the firing stopped, the FBI cordoned off the house while the SWAT TEAM went in. They found Gordon Kahl alive and well inside the home, hiding behind the refrigerator. He was taken to the living room, thrown on the floor, and was worked over with the butt end of their rifles. While numerous bones were being fractured and his teeth were being smashed in, other members of the SWATT TEAM went on a rampage in the house, smashing pictures and the television set, over-turning furniture, a copier, and taking a fireman's axe and chopping up a bookshelf.

While Gordon Kahl was pinned to the floor by the SWATT TEAM, still under attack from the gun butts, the FBI agent with the fireman's axe turned to Gordon Kahl himself and chopped off his hand. Then he went around and chopped off Gordon Kahl's other hand, and then both of his feet were severed. While screaming with pain and with blood gushing out profusely over the floor where his hands and feet used to be, Gordon Kahl was shot in the head at close range, killing him.

A local Deputy Sheriff was given the honour of removing the bullet from Gordon Kahl's head. When local people viewed Gordon Kahl's dismembered body, they became nauseous and sick, stating that the man they just hacked apart was not Gordon Kahl, but Mr. William Wade, who was the owner of the land and resembled Gordon Kahl closely in age and appearance, and was well known to the Sheriff and others personally.

There was total confusion; immediately there was trouble. A massive series of roadblocks were erected again, and the thorough searching of all automobiles over a wide radius was started; it was believed that Gordon Kahl had slipped out once again.

Local residents monitoring the operation on the police radio band heard a call made for some gasoline to be delivered to the house. Now that the murder of Gordon Kahl had been botched, the Feds were going to cover their own tracks and torch the place. The SWATT TEAM left the place with extensive blood stains covering their clothes and took the private FBI jet back to Washington.

The roadblocks were called off when Mr. Wade, the owner of the land, showed up in town alive and well. The body of Sheriff Matthews was taken to a local hospital, while later in the evening after the fire the Feds had set had died down, the charred body of Gordon Kahl was taken to the local coroner.

The dismembered body was later identified as being that of Gordon Kahl. But the bodies and the house were only lightly charred, since the house was fabricated from cast concrete walls and the fire never got that intense. The corpse identified as being Gordon Kahl's was missing teeth, hands, and feet, had a bullet hole in the head without a bullet, and was extensively covered with tissue bruises and fractured bones. It was very shocking and disgusting, as people who saw photographs of Gordon Kahl's charred remains, taken by the coroner, reported a stark and terrified look on his charred face; he had died in extreme terror, screaming violently from the pain.

The man who was Director of the FBI at the time that this murder operation was being performed, was William Webster. He personally supervised it.

Gordon Kahl was later buried with military honours -- whatever that meant.

His wife back in North Dakota received several mean and ugly death threats from the Feds to keep quite about the state of her husband's body or be murdered herself. Meanwhile, the rest of the country went on like Alice strolling through Wonderland; believing that all was well and that the Federal Government is your trusted friend, and that some little Tax Protestor over there got what he deserved.

Back in Arkansas, while shifting through the smouldering ruins in the kitchen, a reporter for the New York Times accompanied by Ray Wade, the land owner's son, found Gordon Kahl's left foot that had been severed off by the axe.

It was taken to the local coroner Dr. Fahmy Malak in Little Rock, confirmed as being Gordon Kahl's sliced off foot. However, this was news not fit to emphasize, and the reporter's story was redacted when printed in the New York Times story "Gunfight Shatters Tranquility of Arkansas Hills", page 14, July 3rd, 1983.

Mr. and Mrs. Ginter, who had been harbouring Gordon Kahl, were charged not only with aiding and abetting a fugitive, but also were fraudulently charged with the murder of Sheriff Matthews. At Trial, the only evidence introduced against them, outside of the background story, was first person evidence from Art Russell's daughter, Karen Russell Robertson, who reported to the Jury that she had seen her father harbour Kahl, and with that eyewitness evidence, the Ginters and Art Russell were convicted and sentenced to life in prison. Incidentally, Mr. Ray Wade, who found Gordon Kahl's foot, was also threatened with being killed himself if he did not remain silent, as were other local residents who also saw different aspects of the bloody reign of FBI terror that went on during that fateful era.

CHEVIE O'BRIEN KEHOE

Born January 19th 1973 – sentenced to life in prison June 25th, 1999. Executed July 14th, 2020.

Chevie Kehoe, his father, Kirby Kehoe, his brother Cheyne Kehoe, co-defendant Daniel Lee, and Faron Lovelace were involved in a variety of criminal activities to promote and fund a white supremacist organization founded by Kehoe, known as the Aryan Peoples' Republic and the Aryan Peoples' Resistance (APR).
Kehoe envisioned that APR would succeed where the Order, a previous white supremacist organisation, had failed. APR would establish an independent country in the Pacific Northwest of the USA composed only of white members of the Christian Identity faith. The population would be maintained through the practice of polygamy and by the recruitment of people with similar beliefs, such as that Jewish people are the devil's lineal descendants and that white members of Christian Identity are the chosen ones.
In February 1995, Kehoe and his father robbed the Arkansas home of William Mueller, a formerly licensed gun dealer who owned a large collection of weapons and ammunition. Kehoe and his family transported the stolen property, which included guns, gun-parts, ammunition, and gun-related merchandise, from Mueller's home in Tilley, Arkansas, to the Shadows Motel in Spokane, Washington, by way of the Christian Identity community in Elohim City, Oklahoma, where Kehoe met Lovelace who joined them..
In June 1995, Kehoe and Lovelace kidnapped and robbed Malcolm and Jill Friedman, a Jewish couple, who owned a store in Coleville, Washington, at which Kehoe had

once been employed. Kehoe and Lovelace robbed the Friedmans of more than $15,000. Kehoe retained the majority of the money and distributed the remainder to Lovelace and Kirby Kehoe. Both Kehoe and Lovelace bought property near Priest River, Idaho, with their respective portions of the proceeds from the kidnapping and robbery.

In January 1996, Kehoe and Lee returned to the Mueller's Arkansas property posing as federal agents. The two men overpowered William Mueller, his wife Nancy, and her eight-year-old daughter Sarah Powell from a previous marriage. After incapacitating William and Nancy, Kehoe and Lee questioned Sarah Powell regarding the location of the approximately $50,000 Mueller had in his possession. After taking Mueller's money, as well as coins and firearms, Kehoe and Lee placed plastic bags over all three victims' heads and affixed the bags to their bodies with duct tape. After weighting the bodies with rocks and binding them further with duct tape, Kehoe and Lee threw them into the Illinois Bayou. The corpses were discovered in Lake Dardanelle near Russellville, Arkansas, in late June 1996.

Kehoe and Lee returned to Spokane, Washington, around January 14th, 1996, with property stolen from the Muellers. Over the next few months, Kehoe moved about the country frequently. He travelled to his parents' residence in Yaak, Montana. He and Cheyne then travelled to Arizona, and then to Texas. In all of these states, Kehoe, as well as other members of his family, sold off Mueller's guns and property. While in Texas, Kehoe confessed his role in the Mueller murders to his brother Cheyne, telling him that he and Lee wore federal officer raid jackets and caps when they ambushed the Muellers and Powell. He then described the manner in which he and Lee killed the family and disposed of their bodies.

On February 15th, 1997, after attending a gun show in Cincinnati, Ohio, Kehoe and Cheyne were stopped by police officers in Wilmington, Ohio. The officer asked Kehoe, who was driving, to provide identification. After Kehoe refused to do so, the officer asked him to step out of the Chevrolet Suburban, at which point Kehoe and Cheyne ran from the officer. Cheyne pulled out a gun and began to fire. Kehoe got back into the vehicle and drove away in the confusion, leaving Cheyne to flee on foot. Kehoe drove to an industrial park where, shortly afterwards, another team of police officers found the vehicle. As an officer approached it Kehoe fired approximately thirty-three rounds at him and his colleague. Although neither officer was injured seriously, a passer-by was shot in the arm. Kehoe escaped on foot. A search of the Suburban revealed property belonging to the Muellers, along with the federal raid jackets and caps used during the robbery and murders. Both Kehoe and Cheyne stole cars and drove west. Kirby met Cheyne in Wyoming, and Kehoe met his mother, Gloria Kehoe, in South Dakota. The family reunited in Utah.

In June 1997, Cheyne turned himself in to police. He provided the police with paint samples from the Suburban, which matched paint stuck to the duct tape used to bind the Muellers and Powell. Shortly thereafter, Kirby Kehoe was arrested on gun violations, but was released pending trial. Gloria Kehoe, the mother, contacted ATF agents in Spokane, stating that she had begun to fear for her life because "she knew too much." She provided information that led to the discovery of more of the Muellers' property in storage units rented to the Kehoes, including numerous weapons and a key fitting the handcuffs that Mueller was wearing at the time of his death. Gloria also told the officers that both Kehoe and Daniel Lee had confessed to their roles in the Mueller murders. Kehoe, Lee, and Kirby Kehoe were among the APR members indicted on December 12th, 1997. Kirby pleaded guilty and cooperated with authorities. Following a two-month trial, a jury convicted Kehoe and Lee on all five counts of the indictment.

On February 20, 1998, Kehoe pleaded guilty to felonious assault, attempted murder and carrying a concealed weapon related to a February 15th, 1997 shootout in Wilmington, Ohio with an Ohio State Highway Patrol Trooper and a Clinton County sheriff's deputy during a standard traffic stop resulting from expired tags on his 1977 blue Chevrolet Suburban.

Video from the dashboard camera of the patrolman's car can be found on the internet.

In 2005, Kehoe pleaded guilty and was convicted of the murders of the gun dealer Robert Mueller and his family. He received three sentences of life imprisonment without parole. Kehoe's mother Gloria and his younger brother Cheyne served as prosecution witnesses and testified against him at the trial. Kehoe is presently serving his sentence at USP Lee.

Daniel Lee pleaded not guilty to the murders and was sentenced to death and was executed on July 14th, 2020.

Why was Lee executed and Kehoe not?

When Kehoe was sentenced to life imprisonment, federal prosecutors initially planned to pursue a similar sentence of life imprisonment for accomplice Daniel Lewis Lee, but were directed by the United States department of Justice in Washington, D.C., to argue for a death sentence. U.S. Attorney Paula casey requested U.S. Attorney General Janet Reno withdraw jeopardy of capital punishment but was told by Deputy U.S. Attorney General Eric Holder to continue seeking a death sentence. On May 4th, 1999, Lee received a death sentence for three counts of murder in aid of racketeering after the prosecution pointed to his previous convictions as evidence that he was a future danger to society. On July 24th, 1990, in Oklahoma City, Lee got into an altercation with another man, Joseph "Joey" Wavra III, at a party. Lee struck Wavra in the face and kicked him on the floor once he had collapsed. He then assisted his cousin, John David Patton, in moving Wavra to a sewer tunnel. Lee took items from Wavra and handed Patton a knife which Patton used to kill him. Lee then assisted in disposing of Wavra's clothes. On December 2nd, 1990, Lee pleaded guilty to robbery, whereupon the murder charge was dismissed. He received a five-year suspended sentence for his involvement in the crime, while Patton was sentenced to life without parole. Patton died in prison on January 7th, 2014.

It all now gets very legally involved, you have been warned!

In December 1999, the United States court of Appeals for the 8th Circuit issued a writ of mandamus quashing Lee's subpoenas of Reno and Holder regarding the sentencing decision. In March 2000, District Judge Garnet Thomas Eisele granted Lee's motion for a new penalty phase trial if the Attorney General herself decided not to withdraw the death penalty. In December 2001, that judgment was reversed by the Eighth Circuit, which reinstated Lee's death sentence. In July 2004, the Eighth Circuit affirmed Lee's conviction and death sentence on the merits.

In April 2013, the Eighth Circuit affirmed the denial of Lee's Habeas Corpus petition challenging the constitutionality of his conviction. In July 2015, the Eighth Circuit affirmed the denial of Lee's subsequent habeas motion challenging the constitutionality of his prior habeas motion. Lee was scheduled to be executed on December 9th, 2019, and would have been the first inmate to be executed by the federal government since the execution of Louis Jones Jnr. in 2003. On November 20th, 2019, U.S. District Judge Tanya Chutkan issued a preliminary injunction preventing the resumption of federal executions. Lee and the other three plaintiffs in the case argued that the use of pentobarbital may violate the Federal death Penalty Act of 1994.

On December 5th, 2019, an Indiana federal court stayed Lee's execution, but the United States court of Appeals for the 7th Cicuit vacated the Indiana federal court's stay of execution on December 6th, 2019. Later that same day, the Supreme Court of the United states denied a stay of Chutkan's injunction against all federal executions while the U.S. Court of Appeals reviews Chutkan's decision.

In April 2020, a panel of the United States court of Appeals for the Columbia circuit vacated District Judge Chutkan's injunction in a per curiam decision. Circuit Judges Gregory C. Katkas and Neomi Rao both wrote concurring opinions concluding that Lee may be executed, but for different reasons. Circuit Judge David S. Tatel dissented, arguing that the statute explicitly requires the federal government to follow state execution protocols. On June 29th, 2020, the Supreme Court denied Lee's petition for a writ of certiorari, with Justices Ruth Bader Ginsburg and Sonia Sotomayor dissenting.

The execution date was set for July 13th, 2020, the first of several federal executions scheduled after the D.C. Circuit's ruling. The victims' families asked for a rescheduling of the date, saying they were unable to travel to witness the execution due to the COVID-19 pandemic, but the Seventh Circuit ruled that while allowing the victims' families to attend such events is standard practice, there are no rights or legal basis for their attendance, and denied a change in date. The victims' families sent an emergency appeal to the Supreme Court. Before the Supreme Court could rule, Judge Chutkan ordered a halt to all federal executions on the basis that the process was "very likely to cause extreme pain and needless suffering". The Department of Justice appealed to both the Court of Appeals for the D.C. Circuit and the Supreme Court. The D.C. Circuit Court did not intervene. In the early morning of July 14th, 2020, the Supreme Court lifted the hold that Judge Chutkan previously implemented in a 5–4 decision. This action allowed the Department of Justice to proceed with the execution; Lee's lawyers said that the execution could not go forward after midnight under federal regulations.

Lee was executed later that morning. When asked for a final statement, he denied committing the crime, stating, "I didn't do it. I've made a lot of mistakes in my life, but I'm not a murderer. You're killing an innocent man", and that he and Kehoe had been in a different part of the country when the crime occurred. Lee was pronounced dead at 8:07 a.m. after receiving a single-dose lethal injection of pentobarbital.

DANIEL LEWIS LEE

Born January 31st 1973 – executed by lethal injection July 14th, 2020
See under CHEVIE O'BRIEN KEHOE

JESSIE MISKELLEY

Born July 10th, 1975 – sentenced to life plus 40 yeras February 4th, 1994.

A.K.A. one of THE WEST MEMPHIS THREE.

See under JAMES BALDWIN.

ABDULHAKIM MUJAHID MUHAMMAD
Born **Carlos Leon Bledsoe**

Born July 9th 1985 – sentenced to life in prison without parole July 25th, 2011.

Abdulhakim Mujahid Muhammad, previously known as Carlos Leon Bledsoe, was born on July 9th, 1985 in Memphis, Tennessee to Melvin Bledsoe, a businessman, and his wife Linda. He has a sister Monica. Raised as a Baptist and considered a bright child, he graduated from Craigmont High School in Memphis in 2003. He attended Tennessee State University in Nashville, Tennessee, for three semesters.

At the age of 19, Bledsoe converted to Islam in 2004 at Masjid As-Salam, a Memphis mosque. He has said "I've loved jihad ever since I became Muslim." He became more devout and prayed regularly at the Islamic Centre of Nashville, wearing Arab-style clothing. By 2007 he was a deeply religious Muslim and had legally changed his name to Muhammad.

In 2007, Muhammad travelled to visit Yemen and stayed there for about 16 months, ostensibly to teach English at an institute called The British Academy, and other places in Aden and Sana'a and to learn Arabic to further his understanding of Islam.

While there, in September 2008 he married Reena Abdullah Ahmed Farag, a woman from South Yemen who worked as an elementary school teacher. She was left behind when he was deported back to the U.S.A but he later sent for her.

In his handwritten letters of May to October 2010, Muhammad claimed to have known people in Yemen who "showed him around and helped him get started," but didn't say who they were or how he met them, declining to do so for what he referred to as "security reasons."

He claimed to have been "asked many times to carry out a martyrdom operation in America", but "didn't have proper training in regards to explosives." He said he tried to travel to Somalia for weapons and bomb-making training, particularly car-bomb-making. He wrote in 2010, "Had I got this training my story would have ended a lot differently than it's going to end now. My drive-by would have been a drive-in, with no one escaping the aftermath."

Muhammad was arrested at a roadside checkpoint in Yemen on November 14th, 2008. He had overstayed his visa, lacked the proper government permissions to travel, and was holding a fraudulent Somali passport. In his car were found explosive manuals that included tips such as how to make gun silencers, literature by Anwar Al-Awlaki (the late cleric in Yemen linked to Al-Qaeda in the Arabian Peninsula), videos and literature about "Muslim soldiers in different parts of the world", and "people's numbers on my phone that were wanted in Saudi Arabia."

Imprisoned for over two months in Yemen, Muhammad said in his account that he was "maybe insulted in interrogation a few times, but not tortured". He began planning to carry out jihad against the U.S. while he was in prison. James E. Hensley Jr., Muhammad's American lawyer after his arrest in the United States, later said that he was radicalized by Islamic fundamentalists while in prison.

Under pressure from the United States, Yemen deported Muhammad to the U.S. on January 29th, 2008. Because his original plan to travel to Somalia for bomb training had been foiled by his arrest in Yemen, Muhammad said he revised his plan "with the help of the Mujahideen", the Al-Qaeda in the Arabian Peninsula (AQAP). Investigators have not independently confirmed his claims.

After his return, Muhammad initially stayed with his parents in Memphis. He moved to Little Rock, Arkansas in April, where his father opened an office to provide a job for his son and a chance for him to bring his wife from Yemen. His parents ran a successful tour bus business "Twin City Tours", and he worked for his father as a driver.

After his return, Muhammad was investigated by the FBI's Joint Terrorism Task Force. The Task Force also investigated the suspect's visit to Columbus, Ohio; authorities had monitored some Somali Americans travelling from there to Somalia to "wage jihad."

On June 1st, 2009 Muhammad drove by the Little Rock U.S. Army recruiting centre at 9112 North Rodney Parham Road near Reservoir Road in a black 2003 Ford Explorer Sport Trac at 10:19 a.m. Private William Andrew "Andy" Long, 23, of Conway, Arkansas, and Private Quinton I. Ezeagwula, 18, of Jacksonville, Arkansas, were standing outside the recruiting centre in uniform, smoking cigarettes. Muhammad saw them, approached, stopped his vehicle, and shot them with an SKS rifle. The two victims had just completed their basic training two weeks prior, and volunteered to work as recruiters, which was not their regular assignment.

A witness, Lance P. Luplow, heard approximately seven loud bangs and then saw a black truck with tinted windows speeding away, with its tailgate down spilling bottles of water onto the street. Luplow ran to Long, who had been shot several times, and was lying still in a pool of blood on the sidewalk. Ezeagwula was crawling to the door, holding a bloodied ear. Ezeagwula exclaimed: "Tell me this isn't real, tell me this isn't real". Other soldiers came to treat them and performed CPR on Long. Long was dead upon arrival at a hospital. Ezeagwula, who was shot in his back, head, and buttocks, was rushed into surgery at Baptist Hospital in critical condition.

Long's father later remarked: "They weren't on the battlefield; but apparently, the battlefield's here."

Muhammad sped away, planning to drive 150 miles to Memphis, Tennessee, where he intended to switch cars. After a short pursuit by police patrol cars, he took a wrong turn in a construction zone, and local police officers captured him eight miles from the recruiting centre, near the intersection of Interstate 30 and Interstate 630 at downtown Little Rock. He surrendered to Little Rock police officers without incident.

He stepped out of his SUV, wearing a green ammo belt. He said: "It's a war going on against Muslims, and that is why I did it". He used language "indicating an association with jihad", and claimed that he had explosives, but none were found.

He was found to be in possession of an SKS rifle, a Mossberg International 702 rifle with scope and laser sight, a .22 calibre handgun, a Lorcin L-380 semi-automatic handgun, 562 rounds of ammunition loaded in magazines, homemade sound suppressors, binoculars, a "suspicious" package, and two military books. A police search of his apartment turned up Molotov cocktails, homemade sound suppressors, and compact discs labelled with Arabic writing.

He was indicted on one count of capital murder and 15 counts of terrorist acts. He was charged with capital murder, attempted capital murder and 10 counts of unlawful discharge of a weapon. Prosecutors sought the death penalty.

He was held in the Pulaski County Detention Centre, awaiting a scheduled February 2011 jury trial. In January 2010, Arkansas Judge Herbert Wright ordered the State's Public Defenders Commission to pay part of the bill for Muhammad's private attorney. That same month, in a two-page, handwritten letter to the judge in his case, Muhammad changed his plea to guilty. For the first time, he claimed to be a "soldier in Al-Qaeda in the Arabian Peninsula" (AQAP), and described the recruiting office shooting as a "Jihadi attack." He said he was part of Abu Basir's Army, a reference to Naser Abdel-Karim al-Wahishi, the AQAP leader in Yemen. Muhammad affirmed that his sanity was intact, and that he was acting of his own volition in changing his plea.

Muhammad's father said he doubted whether his son had any such ties or affiliations and described his son as 'being unable to process reality' and being so 'brainwashed' as to want to tie his act to the terrorist group so that he could face execution and become a martyr.

Muhammad was found guilty and sentenced to whole life in prison without parole on July 25th, 2011.

ERIC RANDALL NANCE

Born January 9th, 1960 – executed by lethal injection in Arkansas November 29th, 2005.

Eighteen year old Julie Heath was last seen alive on October 11th, 1993 when she left her home in Malvern, Arkansas that evening to visit her boyfriend in Hot Springs, Arkansas. Julie's car broke down on the way. Eric Nance was returning to Malvern from Hot Springs in his pickup at this time. When he left Hot Springs, he was dressed in a shirt, bib-overalls, and shoes. According to Nance, he stopped to help and offered Julie a ride to Malvern. He was later seen in a convenience store with no shoes, socks, or shirt. He also had dark, damp stains on his overalls that appeared to be fresh.

Julie's car was found abandoned on Highway 270, west of Malvern on the 12th. A week later on October 18th, 1993, her body was found in a wooded area just off an unpaved road about seven miles from her car. The body was fully clothed. A photograph of the clothed body that was admitted into evidence at Nance's later trial shows that the belt buckle was partially undone; the pants' zipper was partially zipped; and the portion of the shirt covering the body's right shoulder was torn.

An officer testified at trial that the shirt was inside out when the body was found. And photographs of the shirt once it was removed from the body reveal that the shirt's torn shoulder was its left shoulder. The officer also testified that he concluded the shirt was wrong-side out because when he saw the clothed body in the woods, the shirt's shoulder pad was on the outside surface of the garment. The shirt's other shoulder pad was found nearby.

The medical examiner testified that when the body was presented to him it was dressed in one black shirt which was inside out, one pair of black jeans, one black belt, one pair of black socks, which were inside out, one pair of black shoes, a white bra, which was pulled up around the neck and shoulder area, pink panties, which were inside out. The shirt and pants were intact around the body. The belt was buckled and the zipper was partially zipped. The medical examiner also testified that the shirt was torn or cut near the shoulder.

A search of Nance's pickup revealed red pubic hairs in the cab. Julie had red hair and an expert testified that these hairs were microscopically similar to some taken from Julie's body. Nance's defence theory was that he accidentally killed Julie. He claimed that when she was riding in his pickup she saw his box-cutter knife when he went to move it from his trouser pocket to the glove compartment as it was uncomfortable when driving and she became hysterical, kicking him and pulling his hair, and that he put up his hand that held the knife to make her stop and claimed that after he put his hand up, he realized the knife had become lodged in her throat. Though Nance did not testify, this version of his story arose at trial through his brother and sister, to whom he had told the same story.

In the guilt phase of the trial, the jury found Nance guilty of capital felony murder with attempted rape as the underlying felony. In the sentencing phase, the State presented as evidence six prior felony convictions stemming from Nance's rape and beating of two Oklahoma girls in 1982. Nance was released from his twenty-year sentence for those convictions just five months before he killed Julie.

The jury found that two statutory aggravating circumstances existed beyond a reasonable doubt, that no mitigating circumstances existed, that the aggravating circumstances outweighed any mitigating circumstances beyond a reasonable doubt, and that "the aggravating circumstances justify beyond a reasonable doubt the sentence of death." The judge, following the jury's recommendation, sentenced Nance to death.

Twelve years later after exhausting his appeals and being refused clemency Eric Nance was executed by lethal injection on November 29th, 2005.

RILEY DOBI NOEL

Born May 22nd, 1972 – executed by lethal injection in Arkansas on July 9th, 2003.

In the early morning hours of June 5th, 1995, Marcell Young, 17, Malak Hussian, 10, and Mustafa Hussian, 12 -- all siblings -- were shot and killed in their home while their mother, Mary Hussian, wrestled with another gunman in a separate part of the house.

In an information filed on July 5th, 1995, the prosecutor charged Riley Noel, Carroll, Curtis Lee Cochran, and Tracy Trinette Calloway with the capital murders of the three children and the attempted capital murder of Mary Hussian.

On June 4th, 1995, Noel, Carroll, Cochran and Calloway were riding around Little Rock in Cochran's car, high on drugs. They went to the home of Mary Hussian, where Calloway got out of the car and followed Noel and Carroll to the house.

Just before they entered the house, Noel handed Calloway a handgun, and she testified that she returned it immediately. Noel burst into the house, and Calloway followed, stopping just inside the doorway. Noel told three children in the residence to get down on the floor, and Calloway testified that she told them to do what Noel said. She watched Noel shoot each of the children in the head and kill them.

According to Curtis Cochran, the murders were in retaliation for the death of Noel's brother. Noel believed that another child of Mary Hussian, a daughter, had been involved in his brother's drive-by shooting death.

Following the murders, Calloway testified that she ran from the house with Carroll. According to police records, Noel shot Hussian's 3 children, ages 10, 12 and 17, as they lay on the living room floor.

Carroll tried to shoot the mother with a shotgun in another room but it jammed, and she was able to wrestle it away from him. Prosecutors argued that Noel, 24, killed the children to avenge his brother's slaying, which had occurred about a week earlier. Police said Noel believed one of Hussian's daughters had set up his brother's death in the drive-by shooting.

Tracy Calloway gave a full statement indicating that she was with the young men at the time of the murders but stating that she was not aware of an intention to commit the killings. A defence she repeated at her trial.

But the prosecutor presented testimony from Curtis Cochran, who was driving the vehicle that day who testified that everyone in the car knew where they were going and what Noel intended to do because Noel announced it in the car.

According to Cochran, Noel gave Tracy Calloway a .45 calibre handgun while they were in the car, and she still had it in her hand when they went to the Hussian house.

Jack Thomas, a neighbour of the victims, also testified for the State and stated that he saw Calloway run from the Hussian house and that it appeared as though she was carrying a gun.

Kyle Jones testified that he arrived at the Hussian residence with his fiancé, Marcel Young, and saw three people standing in the carport: Noel, Cochran, and Calloway.

The threesome asked Marcel and Kyle if Yashica Young was home, and Kyle said that he would check. Kyle and Marcel entered the house, and Kyle went to the back of the home to tell Marcel's mother, Mary Hussian, that they were home.

He heard someone burst in through the front of the house and heard Marcel scream. Kyle and Mary Hussian ran toward the front of the house and were intercepted by Carroll, who was carrying a shotgun.

They retreated to the bedroom. Kyle went into the bathroom and closed the door. Mary Hussian hid behind the bed and called 911. Kyle testified that he heard three shots come from the front room and that he heard the shotgun blast in the bedroom just before he escaped through the window.

Kyle eventually came back to the house and told police officers what he had seen. Mary Hussian told the same story to the jury as Kyle did. She testified that when she hid behind the bed to call 911, Carroll yelled for her to come out from behind the bed. She pleaded with him not to kill her or her children.

She eventually rushed Carroll, and they fought for control of the shotgun. The shotgun discharged in the struggle, and the shot went through the roof. Mary Hussian gained control of the gun and chased Carroll back through the house, where she saw her three murdered children lying on the floor.

Carroll left through the front door. Mary Hussian saw three people in the house, but could only identify Carroll and Noel and not Calloway.

The State also contended at trial that Calloway's original statement to the Little Rock police officers and her trial testimony conflicted with each other.

She first told police officers that she was in the car and that Cochran picked up Carroll and Noel, but at trial she testified that the threesome picked her up to give her a ride home. She also testified at trial that she did not see any guns in the car until the group was about to go into the Hussian house.

However, it was established at the trial by forensic analysis that two weapons were used at the murder scene -- a .45 calibre pistol and a shotgun. Calloway admitted that Carroll was in the back seat of the two-door car with her but maintained that she did not see the shotgun. Calloway was sentenced to a total term in prison of 132 years. Cochran testified for the state and received 20 years, Carroll got life.

Noel was tried and convicted on three charges of first degree murder and sentenced to death. Despite his lawyers putting forward medical evidence of severe brain deficiencies during his appeals and clemency petition the sentence was upheld and he was executed by lethal injection at the Cummins Unit of the Arkansas Department of Corrections on July 9th, 2004.

TERRICK TERRELL NOONER

Born March 17th, 1971 – sentenced to death September 28th, 1993.

On March 16th, 1993, at approximately 1:30 a.m. Scot Stobaugh entered the FunWash laundromat on West Markham Street in Little Rock to do his laundry. While there, he was shot seven times and died of multiple gunshot wounds. He was found lying face down on the laundromat floor in a pool of blood. Subsequent examination showed that he was shot twice in the upper right arm and five times in the back in what later were described as contact wounds. Seven .22 calibre shell casings were found on the floor close to the body together with a tan hat, keys, and a jar of Carmex lip salve. His Chevrolet Beretta was parked in the laundromat's parking area unlocked, with its parking lights on, and with the keys in the ignition. A ring and a neck band remained on the victim's body.

The FunWash laundromat had three surveillance cameras in operation at the time of the shooting which recorded on one VHS videotape. The general manager of the business, Janie White, helped investigating police officers from the Little Rock Police Department retrieve the videotape. The videotape depicted Stobaugh and a second person accosting him in the laundromat. It did not show the actual murder.

Detective Joe Oberle, a homicide detective with the Little Rock Police Department, took possession of the videotape and had still photographs made from the frames that included the victim and the suspect. Detective Oberle used several private firms in Little Rock to enhance the tape in order to obtain the clearest still pictures possible, Color Masters, Camera Mart, and Jones Productions. In four of the enhanced photographs, the victim's face was "mosaicked out" at the request of his family and one of those photographs was given to the news media to assist in the investigation for the killer.

Ron Andrejack, the firearms examiner for the State Crime Laboratory, examined the bullets and shell casings found at the crime scene and determined that five of the seven bullets were fired by the same firearm. The other two bullets were too damaged for any conclusion to be reached. He further determined that all seven shell casings were fired from the same gun. By examining the various marks on the bullets and shell casings, he ultimately concluded that the characteristics on the bullets and shell casings were consistent with a .22 Ruger semi-automatic pistol.

In a matter of days, the police investigation had centred on Nooner due in large part to statements given to Detective Oberle by Antonia "Toni" Kennedy, a friend of Nooner's. Antonia Kennedy is the sister of Jazmar Kennedy, who identified Nooner in the surveillance photographs at trial, and the sister of Terri Kennedy, who was Nooner's girlfriend at the time of the trial and who testified as a defence witness. Antonia Kennedy implicated Nooner in the FunWash shooting and subsequently testified at his trial that on the morning after the shooting Nooner told her that he had murdered Scot Stobaugh after demanding money from him. She added that she had seen Nooner with a .22 Ruger pistol that day and had kept the gun for Nooner for a brief period of time. Nooner was arrested on April 23rd, 1993, and charged with capital murder, aggravated robbery, and theft of property.

On September 20th, 1993, a seven-day trial commenced. Nooner was convicted of capital felony murder with aggravated robbery and theft of property as the underlying felonies. After the penalty phase of the trial, the jury found two aggravating circumstances: (1) that Nooner had previously committed another felony, an element of which was the use or threat of violence; and (2) that the murder was committed for pecuniary gain. The jury found no mitigating circumstances and returned a verdict of death by lethal injection.

Twice Nooner's execution date has been set and twice a Stay has been granted. His appeals continue with the latest based on the confession by another prisoner serving time for murder stating he was the one who killed Scot Stobaugh 31 years ago.

WILLIAM FRANK PARKER

Born 1954 – executed by lethal injection August 8th, 1996.

Soon after William Parker and Pam Warren divorced, Parker approached the home of Pam Warren's parents, James and Sandra Warren, he was dressed in combat fatigues and carrying a 9mm pistol. When James Warren and daughter Cindy Warren left the house, Parker attacked. Cindy managed to spray mace at Parker, ran towards a neighbour's house, and escaped. Parker followed James Warren into the house, where he shot and killed both James and Sandra Warren. Parker then abducted Pam Warren from her apartment and took her to a police station, where he shot and seriously wounded her and a police officer before fleeing and surrendering several hours later.

Parker was convicted of capital felony murder and sentenced to death for killing James and Sandra Warren. The Arkansas Supreme Court reversed the verdict because the killings were not committed during the course of an independent felony. The State then retried Parker for the Warren homicides, this time charging him with premeditated capital murder. He was again convicted and sentenced to death which the Arkansas Supreme Court affirmed on direct appeal.

Parker then commenced his federal habeas appeal proceedings, raising nine claims.

During the time taken for his appeals Parker adopted Buddism and attracted support from the Dalai Lama who wrote to oppose his execution and the actor Richard Gere who hoped to visit him on death row prior to his execution.

Gere's visit was refused as the Corrections Department said it didn't have the time to do a background check on Gere.

William Parker was executed by lethal injection in Arkansas on August 8th, 1996.

EUGENE WALLACE PERRY

Born 1944 – executed by lethal injection in Arkansas on August 6th, 1997.

Sometime in the late afternoon of September 10th, 1980, someone robbed the Staton Jewellery Store in Van Buren, Arkansas, of an estimated $100,000 worth of rings, watches and other jewellery, and shot to death the owner of the store, Kenneth Staton, and his daughter, Suzanne Ware, who also worked in the store. A clerk at a neighbouring store in the same Cloverleaf shopping Centre in Van Buren discovered the two bound and gagged bodies in the rear part of the store at around 6:00 p.m. Autopsies revealed that both Ware and her father had been shot twice in the head ar close range.

Key witnesses for the state placed Eugene Wallace Perry, in and around the Staton Jewellery Store on several occasions preceding the robbery and murders. At least seven other people identified Perry as a man that they had seen in the Van Buren area during a period surrounding the 10th of September, 1980. In addition, various pieces of physical evidence collected would connect Perry to the jewellery store and the September 10th, 1980, murders. The Court at his later trial set forth all of the evidence in some detail.

Ruth Staton, the wife and mother of the victims, testified that she saw Perry in the Staton Jewellery Store on September 3rd, 1980, one week before the robbery. She stated the man she believed to be Perry remained in the store looking at the display cases for over 30 minutes, affording her an opportunity to observe him. Mrs. Staton testified that the man was there with a woman and that she noted this man conspicuously kept his hands tucked under his arms or in his pockets.

Two other local merchants testified that Perry had been in their stores on September 9th, 1980, one day before the crime. Arthur Parr said that Perry was one of two men who entered his jewellery store in Fort Smith, Arkansas on September 9th, 1980. According to Parr, both men carried motorcycle helmets and they looked at the store's merchandise for about 15 minutes. Another witness, Walter Carson, told of a similar episode involving two men, travelling on a motorcycle, who came into Paul's Pawn Shop on September 9th, 1980. Carson stated that the two men told him that they were gold buyers. He identified Perry as one of these men. He believed that this man's name was "Anderson" because he had produced a Kansas driver's license bearing that name. The State's Exhibit 22 was a pawn ticket issued by Carson to 'Anderson' on September 10th, 1980, when the latter pawned a ring for $45.00.

Crucial testimony was offered by Chantina Ginn. She testified that sometime after the first of September 1980, she and a man named Rick Anderson travelled from Kansas to Arkansas on a blue Harley-Davidson motorcycle, which she identified as the one shown to her in photographs in State's Exhibits 13, 14, and 15. Ginn stated that they went to the Horseshoe Bend camping area on Beaver Lake near Rogers, Arkansas. There, according to Ginn, she and Anderson met a man named Damon Peterson and his apparent wife, Lorili Peterson, who were camped at an adjacent campsite.

Ginn testified that the Petersons had a white camper trailer, which they were pulling behind a light blue Cadillac, and that they invited Rick Anderson and her to stay with them in the camper. She further noted that this camper had a cardboard license plate with the words "Lost Tag" handwritten on it. Ginn identified State's Exhibits 27 and 28 at Perry's trial as photographs of the Petersons' camper and State's Exhibits 44-46 as photographs of the Cadillac that pulled the camper.

Ginn stated that on or about the third day after the two couples had met, which would have been either the 8th or 9th of September, Rick and Damon left on the motorcycle, taking with them a briefcase with a gun inside it, a change of clothes, some rope, and a woman's brown wig. She testified that when the two men returned several nights later, they had two orange duffle bags of jewellery which they spread out on the floor of the camper and proceeded to divide among the four individuals.

The following day September 11th, Anderson and Peterson traded the blue Cadillac for another car, according to Ginn's testimony. She said that the four later burned their trash at the campsite, including some jewellery tags and watch boxes that had been left on the floor of the camper the night before. The four then left the Horseshoe Bend camping area and went to a storage facility in Fayetteville, Arkansas where Ginn stated that they placed the motorcycle and the camper in a self-storage room before leaving the state enroute to Atlanta. Finally, Ginn identified Perry as the man whom she had known as Damon Peterson and with whom she and Rick had camped at Beaver Lake.

Pat Etier also testified that an individual known to her as Damon Peterson was one and the same person as Eugene Perry. Etier stated that she saw Perry and another man, who was introduced to her as "Rick," on the afternoon of September 9th, 1980 at the Walmart parking lot in Van Buren. She said the two men were riding a Harley-Davidson motorcycle when she saw them. She identified State's Exhibits 13 and 14 as photographs of that motorcycle, the same photographs which Ginn had identified as being the motorcycle that Anderson and Perry were riding when they left Beaver Lake.

Etier said that she and the two men left the parking lot to get a drink together. She testified that when the man named Peterson climbed into her truck and took off his motorcycle helmet, she noticed that a wig he was wearing came off inside the helmet. She said that this wig was a light brown woman's wig.

After the three had drunk some beer at Peterson's and Anderson's room they had rented at the Terry Motel in Fort Smith, Arkansas, Etier left. But, according to her testimony, she later returned to pick up Perry and took him to her house where they spent the night of September 9th, 1980, together. The following morning, September 10th, Etier drove Perry back to the motel. This occurred around 8:00 a.m. The cities of Fort Smith and Van Buren are immediately adjacent to each other, simply across the river from each other.

Linda Godwin, another important witness, told the jury that she had seen two men walking briskly across the Cloverleaf Shopping Centre parking lot in Van Buren shortly before 6:00 p.m. on September 10th, 1980. Godwin testified that as she was leaving her office she saw two men who appeared to be in a hurry. She identified Perry as one of these two men.

A Mr. Billy Miller testified he saw two men driving a Jeep a few minutes after the robbery. The Jeep apparently belonged to one of the victims.

Grant Cummins supported Chantina Ginn's testimony which placed Perry at the Horseshoe Bend campground.

Cummins said that he was camping on Beaver Lake in early September and that he had talked for several hours with two couples. He identified one of the group as being Perry.

Michael Jeffcoat told the jury that he had sold a used car to a man on September 11th, 1980 in Rogers, Arkansas. Jeffcoat identified Perry as the man who had traded a blue Cadillac for the car Jeffcoat sold him. Jeffcoat testified that he soon sold the Cadillac on to a salvage yard. Police located a blue Cadillac at an auto salvage yard, the same car that was pictured in one of the exhibits that Chantina Ginn identified as the vehicle Perry drove to Beaver Lake.

The search of the car led to the discovery of a single page of the Van Buren telephone book with Kenneth Staton's phone number on it, along with a copy of the September 11th, 1980 edition of the Northwest Arkansas Morning Times headlining the Staton robbery and murders.

The owner of a Fayetteville self-storage facility, Gifford Heckathorn, provided a lease agreement which he said he entered into on September 11th, 1980 with a man who signed as "Damon Peterson" on the contract. Peterson was with another man according to Heckathorn when he rented space No. 109 for a month. Heckathorn testified that he could not say which man signed the agreement. Authorities later opened this storage room and discovered a blue Harley-Davidson motorcycle and white camper trailer. The camper had a cardboard license with "Lost Tag" written on it.

Items found inside the camper underscored the link between the camper and the robbery. From the camper the police obtained the following pieces of physical evidence which were introduced at the trial: a gold coin like those taken from the Staton jewellery store; a buffalo nickel with an identifiable nick on its face and one that Ruth Staton testified she had kept in the store, State's Exhibit 21; a jewellery price tag containing the handwriting of Karen Staton, State's Exhibit 35; a brown plastic ring plug like those used at Staton's to fill up the space in a display case after a ring is sold, State's Exhibit 33; an orange blossom ring filler, State's Exhibit 37; a book of matches from the restaurant at the Terry Motel in Fort Smith, State's Exhibit 30; a book of matches from the Horseshoe Bend Marina in Rogers, Arkansas.

Larry Gray of the Corps of Engineers was the Park Technician at Beaver Lake in 1980. He testified that a user permit was issued by the Corps to a 'Damon Peterson' on September 6th, 1980 and again on September 8th, 1980. These permits, State's Exhibits 49 and 50, indicated that 'Damon Peterson' was assigned campsite 2-10 on each occasion. An investigation of the area around this particular campsite turned up several additional pieces of physical evidence, further linking the campers to the robbery. Police recovered at campsite 2-9, the one adjacent to the one assigned to Peterson, a jewellery box, a ring box, a watch band display holder, and some rope. A crime lab analyst testified that burned remains of a rope found at the campsite possessed characteristics similar to those of the rope which was removed from the hands and legs of the victims.

Perry went to trial for double murder, was found guilty, sentenced to death and executed on August 6th, 1997, seventeen years after the killings when his appeals were exhausted and a last minute appeal to the Supreme Court was denied.

EDWARD CHARLES PICKENS

Born 1954 – executed by electrocution in Arkansas May 11th, 1994.

Edward Pickens was convicted of capital felony murder in 1976 and was held on death row for almost 18 years before exhausting his appeals and being executed. The case raised several public and judicial worries as he pleaded not guilty to the charges and was executed whilst his accomplice Sherwood Gooch pleaded guilty and got life imprisonment.

On October 20th, 1975, in the afternoon, Pickens, Antonio Clark and Sherwood Gooch entered a rural grocery store in Casscoe, Arkansas, armed with a sawn-off shotgun and a .22 calibre pistol. During the robbery of the store the owner, the female store clerk and seven customers were shot. Two of the robbers sexually assaulted the female store clerk.

After the robbers had made all of the victims lie face down on the floor, they shot them. Seven of the victims were shot in the back of the head with the pistol and several were shot a second time after the shooter reloaded the pistol. Two of the victims died, including Wesley Noble, 76, who had been shot a second time.

Pickens and Clark were dark-complexioned black men; however, Gooch was a light-complexioned, "Spanish-appearing" man. The store owner implicated Pickens and Clark in the shootings. He testified that the dark-complexioned men did the shooting, not the light-complexioned man. Another witness testified, however, that Pickens had the shotgun during the robbery. The female store clerk testified that Pickens had the pistol; however, she did not know whether he fired the shots.

Later that day Memphis police, acting on a tip, chased and stopped a stolen vehicle carrying Pickens, Clark and Gooch. Although the occupants of the car fled, Pickens and Gooch were quickly apprehended. The pistol used in the shootings was thrown away by Pickens as he fled but recovered and proved by ballistic forensics to be the one used in the killings. The car contained items taken during the grocery store robbery. Pickens was found to be wearing the female store clerk's wedding ring when he was arrested.

When Pickens was interrogated by Memphis and Arkansas police officers, he admitted to participating in the grocery store robbery, but he identified Clark as the shooter and denied that he fired any of the shots. He was convicted of capital felony murder and sentenced to death. Proceedings on direct appeal and for state and federal post-conviction relief followed.

All three were found guilty with Antonio Clark sentenced to death, reduced to a life sentence and Vincent Gooch sentenced to life without parole. Both pleaded guilty. Pickens pleaded not guilty saying he did not fire the gun but was convicted and sentenced to death. This threw a spotlight on the usual sentencing procedure that gave life to a guilty of murder confession and the death sentence to a not guilty plea that failed.

Many of the press and media of the day ran stories that Pickens was put to death simply because he pleaded not guilty. Pickens was 40 when he was executed.

RICKY RAY RECTOR

Born January 12th, 1950 – executed by lethal injection in Arkansas on January 24th, 1992.

This case brought to a head the question of the morality of executing somebody who was mentally retarded. The proof that Rector was so impaired was often given by the fact that during his last meal before execution he asked the warder to save the dessert for afterwards. His IQ had been measured at below 70 which was the standard benchmark for determining mental retardation at the time.

On March 21st, 1981, Rector, 31, and some friends drove to a dance hall at Tommy's Old-Fashioned Home-Style Restaurant in Conway. When one of his friends was refused entry after being unable to pay the three dollar cover charge, Rector became incensed and pulled a .38 pistol from his waist band. He fired several shots, wounding two people and killing a third man. The third man, Arthur Criswell, died almost instantly after being struck in the throat and forehead.

Rector fled the scene of the murder in a friend's car and wandered the city for three days, alternately staying in the woods or with relatives. On March 24th, Rector's sister convinced him to turn himself in. Rector agreed to surrender but only to Officer Robert Martin, whom he had known since he was a child.

Officer Martin arrived at Rector's mother's home shortly after three p.m. and began chatting with Rector's mother and sister in the living room. Shortly after, Rector arrived through the back door and greeted Officer Martin. As Officer Martin turned away to continue his conversation with

Mrs. Rector, Ricky Ray Rector drew his pistol from behind his back and fired two shots into Officer Martin, striking him in the jaw and neck. Rector then turned and walked out of the house.

Once he had left his mother's property he hid behind a wall, put his gun to his own temple and fired. Rector was quickly found by other police officers who answered his mother's 911 call and he was rushed to the local hospital. The shot had destroyed Rector's frontal lobe, resulting in what was essentially a self-lobotomy.

Rector survived surgery to his head and was put on trial for the murders of Criswell and Martin. His defence attorneys argued that Rector was not competent to stand trial, but after hearing conflicting testimony from several experts who had examined Rector, Judge George F. Hartje ruled that Rector was competent to stand trial. Rector was convicted on both counts and sentenced to death. Ricky Ray Rector was executed by lethal injection on January 24th, 1992.

DARRYL V. RICHLEY

Born 1950 – executed by lethal injection August 3rd, 1994.
Seen under HOYT CLINES

JACOB D. ROBIDA

Born June 13th, 1987 – died after a shootout with the police February 5th, 2006.

At around midnight on February 2nd, 2006, Jacob Robida entered Puzzles Lounge, a popular gay bar in New Bedford, Massachusetts, 50 miles (80 km) south of Boston. The 18-year-old, dressed in black, proceeded to order a drink using a fake ID indicating he was 23. After downing his first drink, he asked the bartender if the lounge was a gay bar. The bartender confirmed it was. After a second drink Robida walked into the pool lounge and swung an axe at a patron's head, injuring him. Other patrons tackled him and took the weapon off him, then Robida produced a handgun and began shooting, wounding at least three more people.

Robida fled the scene in a green 1999 Pontiac Grand Am to Charleston, West Virginia, where he was joined by Jennifer Rena Bailey and drove southwest. It has been reported that Robida had lived with Bailey in West Virginia in 2004. It is unclear whether Bailey joined him willingly or if she was abducted at gunpoint.

Police logged the crime at the bar as a hate crime and immediately began a manhunt for Robida and raided his mother's home in New Bedford. She told them she had last seen him at 1:00 a.m. on the night of the crime bleeding from the head and that he had left soon after. At the house they found weapons of all types, including axes, knives, handguns and a shotgun. In his bedroom they found "Nazi regalia" and anti-Semitic writings on the walls.

Fearing he may have left Massachusetts, state police contacted the FBI, sparking a nationwide manhunt. Before long, flyers depicting Robida and Bailey were distributed all over Massachusetts.

In the afternoon of February 4th, 2006, Robida's vehicle was seen about 1,500 miles (2,400 km) away in Arkansas, where Jim Sell, a Gassville police officer, initiated a traffic stop at the Brass Door Restaurant parking lot reporting that Bailey was in the car with Robida. After talking with Sell for about half a minute, Robida opened fire with a 9 mm handgun, killing the officer. He then turned onto Arkansas Highway 201 and headed south to Arkana, Arkansas, where he fired at Arkansas State Police Sgt. Van Nowlin. Police pursued him and laid spike strips across the road in front of him; although these flattened his front tyres, they failed to stop the car. Robida fled for about 18 miles down Arkansas Highway 5, where he turned south and drove into the small town of Norfolk. In the middle of town he lost control of the car due to the front tyres jamming against the bodywork and spun round before hitting two parked vehicles and coming to a halt. He then exchanged gunfire with police. During the gunfight, he shot Bailey in the head at point blank range with a Ruger 9 mm semi-automatic pistol, killing her instantly. After Bailey's death, Robida shot himself in the right side of the head in a suicide attempt. He was given first aid at the spot and then flown more than 100 miles to Springfield, Missouri, for medical treatment, where he died of his injuries the next day, February 5th, 2006.

Examination of Robida's MySpace website showed a passion for Neo-Nazism and the group, Insane Clown Posse, known for its violent and dark lyrics. One song in particular mentions attacking people with an axe, similar to Robida's crime at the gay bar.

On February 7th, 2006, Insane Clown Posse released a statement on the Robida attacks. The group's manager Alex Abbiss extended members Violent J and Shaggy 2 Dope's condolences and prayers to the families of the victims, stating "It's quite obvious that this guy had no clue what being a Juggalo (group fan) is all about. If anyone knows anything at all about ICP, then you know that they have never, ever been down or will be down with any racist or bigotry bullshit."

PAUL RUIZ (with Earl Van Denton)

Born 1947 – executed by lethal injection in Arkansas January 8th, 1997.

Paul Ruiz and Earl Van Denton escaped from an Oklahoma prison and embarked on a crime spree that took them across multiple states, including Arkansas. The men were convicted in Arkansas of killing town marshal Marvin Ritchie and park ranger Opal James in Logan County. They were executed at the Cummins Unit of the Arkansas Department of Correction on January 8th, 1997.

At the time of their escape, Ruiz was serving a life sentence for armed robbery, while Van Denton was serving a life sentence for murder. The pair escaped on June 23rd, 1977, whilst working outside the prison as part of a twenty-member crew tasked with tearing down a brick factory near the prison in McAlester, Oklahoma,. They had been placed in an empty building during a lunch break, but the door to the building was not guarded, allowing Ruiz, Van Denton, and Elmer Finin to escape. Two of the guards tasked with supervising the work crew were demoted and suspended after the incident.

The trio fled from the prison into the city of McAlester. The exact timeline for the events that followed is not clear, but it appears that Finin separated from Ruiz and Van Denton shortly after they escaped. Finin was arrested in Hot Springs, Garland County on October 31st, 1977, at a service station where he was employed. He was returned to the Oklahoma State Penitentiary where he died at the prison on October 21st, 1981.

The first murder that police associated with Ruiz and Van Denton's crime spree occurred on June 27th, 1977, when Gerald Tiffee disappeared in Boswell, Oklahoma. However, lack of evidence meant Ruiz and Denton were never charged with his disappearance.

Moving southeast into Louisiana, Ruiz and Denton murdered Jimmy Cockrell near Colfax. Cockrell's body was found on June 28th. It is suspected that on that same day, Ray Jones and Alton Wilson were killed near Franklinton, Louisiana. Their bodies were found in Tiffee's pickup truck which had been driven into and submerged in a flooded gravel pit.

Moving north, the pair entered Arkansas. Whilst driving a stolen car, Ruiz and Van Denton got a flat tyre near Magazine in Logan County. Removing the tyre from the car, the pair began rolling it towards the town to have it repaired. Marvin Ritchie, the town marshal of Magazine, was informed by local citizens of the men's actions, and he drove out to offer them assistance.

Seizing the opportunity to take the marshal's car, the pair kidnapped Ritchie and drove it through Magazine and Blue Mountain where they were spotted in the patrol car with Ritchie handcuffed in the rear seat. Driving towards Ashley Recreation Area on the shore of Blue Mountain Lake, the pair stopped a truck driven by two U.S. Army Corps of Engineers Rangers.

Rangers David Small and Opal James were ordered into the patrol car, and Ruiz and Van Denton drove it into a thickly wooded area. They handcuffed Small and Ritchie together and forced them into the trunk of the patrol car while making James lie on the ground behind the car. Ruiz took Small's watch, and one of the convicts took Ritchie's shirt. Before closing the trunk they shot both Small and Ritchie. Ritchie was struck in the head and killed. Small was hit in the chest and blacked out for a period but regained consciousness. Searchers found the car about five hours later and rescued Small.

Ruiz and Van Denton then took the Corps of Engineers truck and drove south, with James still captive to use as a guide due to his knowledge of the isolated back roads in the area. They abandoned the truck about forty miles from Magazine when it ran out of gas. They then killed James and hiked to Oden, Montgomery Gounty, where they stole another truck.

Using this vehicle, they drove back into Oklahoma and stole a taxi cab in Purcell on July 1st. They killed the driver of the cab, Melvin Short; his body was found in Grady County, Oklahoma. Driving Short's car, the duo drove to Portland, Oregon. They were captured there on July 8th after they had contacted a family member in Oklahoma for some money and food, but the family member instead contacted the authorities, and the pair were waiting on a money transfer at a currency exchange when captured. At the time of their arrest, Van Denton and Ruiz were with a third man, David Christofferson, whom the pair picked up hitchhiking in eastern Oregon. Christofferson was questioned and released.

After weeks of court room legal manoeuvring, the pair were extradited to Arkansas, tried in Booneville, Logan County on capital murder charges, and convicted on April 27th, 1978. During the trial, Small identified the two escapees as the men who had kidnapped and shot him along with Ritchie and James. The jury deliberated for forty minutes before returning the verdict and deliberated for another hour before recommending the death penalty.

The convictions for both men were overturned by the Arkansas Supreme Court, and they were re-tried in 1983 in Morrilton, Conway County. This occurred due to the pre-trial publicity in Logan County, which was deemed to be prejudicial to their case. Once again, the men were convicted and sentenced to death. The death sentences were overturned by the Eighth U.S. Circuit Court of Appeals in 1987, and that phase of the trial was held again. Once again, both men were sentenced to death. Another appeal filed in 1989 to the Eighth Circuit was denied, followed by a final appeal that was also denied on January 3rd, 1997.

Ruiz and Van Denton were executed at the Cummins Unit, Arkansas Department of Correction, Lincoln County, Arkansas on January 8th, 1997 twenty years after the killings. Both Ruiz and Van Denton declined to give final statements. Small was present for the executions but was not allowed to view the proceedings. Van Denton was executed first and was declared dead at 7:09 p.m. Ruiz was executed next and declared dead at 8:00 p.m.

RONALD GENE SIMMONS Sr.

Born July 15th, 1940 - executed by lethal injection June 25th, 1990.

Ronald Gene Simmons was put to death by lethal injection in 1990 yet, the mention of his name around Pope, Yell, or Johnson county Arkansas still sparks fear in the hearts and minds of the locals who remember the news that broke around Christmas, 1987.

Ronald Gene Simmons Sr. was a retired Air Force Sergeant and Viet Nam Veteran. He was well known in Cloudcroft, New Mexico. He was someone most people feared. "He had a beer in his hand all the time. He had one little room he would stay in all the time. It was dark and seemed spooky, and it stunk," said a friend of his daughters.

In 1981 Simmons and his family fled town when he was reported for having sex with his daughter. He was seen giving her more than friendly kisses good-bye each morning and eventually she admitted to a school Counsellor that she was pregnant with his baby. Charges were filed, but eventually dropped as the Simmons family disappeared from the area.

Almost a year later, they surfaced in Dover, Arkansas. Some 15 miles outside town, in a remote and densely wooded area, at the end of a rutted, red-clay drive where two old mobile homes that had been haphazardly connected together to make one large structure. The area was barricaded like a fortress with cinder blocks and a barbed wire fence
. The driveway was dotted with several large "No Trespassing" signs. The road leading to the home was badly rutted and at times impossible to enter when wet or slick

from snow and ice. The yard area, or area which the Simmons children kept mowed, was covered in piles of junk Simmons claimed to be "building materials". There were several junk automobiles up on blocks and in various stages of demolition scattered around the home.

This man and his family lived in this tiny Arkansas town only 1.8 miles in size, with 1,329 people, 529 households, and 372 families – totally unnoticed. His children attended public school, his wife often attended a local Church, and Simmons had worked several jobs in the nearby town of Russellville, Arkansas.

Simmons school age children were never allowed to attend school functions, friends were never allowed to spend a night at the Simmons home, nor were the Simmons children ever allowed to stay over at a friend's home. Yet, this peculiarity went unnoticed.

Later, school officials were interviewed about the Simmons children and only commented on having noticed the children were always clean and ready to catch the bus in the mornings. Although none of the Simmons children excelled in their studies, none drew attention by falling behind either.

There were no records of disciplinary actions for the Simmons children, and their attendance had been near perfect. When teachers were later questioned about the children in their class, most commented that they really didn't know the children well. It seems incredible that these children could have attended such a small school for so long and managed to remain relatively unnoticed and unknown.

Simmons wife, Rebecca, reportedly tried to leave him on several occasions. Witnesses who were interviewed later remarked that they had noticed bruises on Rebecca's face and arms on numerous occasions. Yet, this too, went unreported. The Simmons home had no phone, they never received mail, nor sent mail from their rural box by the side of their driveway.

Then it all happened. Just before Christmas 1987, Ronald Gene Simmons made a conscious decision to kill all the members of his family. On the morning of December 22nd, Simmons drove to the local Walmart and purchased a .22 calibre handgun.

When he returned home, he first bludgeoned and shot his son Gene and his long-suffering wife Rebecca. For a while, he left their bodies laying where they had fallen. He next focused his attention on his 3 year old daughter Barbara. Simmons strangled little Barbara, and wrapped her body in a black plastic trash bag.

After having a beer, Simmons dumped the bodies in the cesspit he had made his children dig in the back yard several days prior. Now Simmons sat back and awaited the return of his other children. When they arrived off the school bus he said he had Christmas presents for them but wanted to give them out one at a time.

Sending all the children to their rooms, Simmons first summoned 17 year old Loretta, the oldest daughter still at home. Simmons strangled and held Loretta under the water in a rain barrel outside the home until she drowned. The three other children, Eddy, Marianne and Becky were all killed in a similar manner, one after another.

Around noon on December 26th, the remaining members of the family arrived at Simmons home for their planned Christmas visit with the family. The first to die was Simmons' son Billy and daughter-in-law Renata, both shot dead as they entered the home, in full view of their son Trae.

Trae was next to be strangled and drowned as Barbara and the other small children had been.

Arriving at the house less than an hour later were, daughter Sheila and her husband Dennis McNulty, and the incestuous daughter Simmons had fathered with Sheila, Sylvia Gale, and the child Sheila and Dennis had together, Michael. Both Sheila and Dennis were shot not long after they entered the house. Simmons' child by his own daughter, the christened Sylvia Gail, was strangled, and finally grandson Michael, in the same manner as the other small children had been put to death.

Simmons laid the bodies of his whole family in neat rows in the living room. All the corpses were covered with coats except that of Sheila, who was laid out as if in a formal "viewing" state, covered by Mrs. Simmons' best tablecloth. The bodies of the two grandsons were wrapped in plastic sheeting and left in abandoned cars at the end of the lane. Simmons soaked all the bodies in kerosene, he said he believed that it would stop the smell coming out of the ground and prevent attracting animals and people.

After going out for a drink in a local bar, Simmons returned home later the evening of the 26th. Apparently oblivious of the corpses lined up around him, Simmons spent the next night and the following Sunday drinking beer and watching television. He drove into the nearby town of Russellville, Arkansas on Monday the 28th, with the .22-calibre pistol he'd purchased days earlier.

Next, Simmons drove to a law office and shot dead a young woman named Kathy Kendrick, age 24, who for some reason he blamed for many of his problems and who had rejected his amorous advances. Simmons then moved on down the street to the Taylor Oil Company where Simmons shot dead a man named J.D. Chaffin, 33 years old, and wounded the owner.

He then drove to a convenience store where he had once worked and shot and wounded two more people. Simmons continued on to yet another office, Woodline Motor Freight Company, where he shot and wounded a woman. That was the end of his killing spree.

Seemingly perfectly calm after that Simmons simply sat in the Freight Company office and chatted to one of the secretaries while waiting for the police. When they arrived he handed over his gun and surrendered without any resistance. No one at the scene that morning guessed Ronald Gene Simmons was actually winding down a killing spree. What appeared to be a contained incident of workplace violence was far worse. In fact, it had set a record.

Simmons was charged with sixteen counts of murder, found guilty and sentenced to death. On May 31st, Arkansas Governor, later president Bill Clinton, signed Simmons execution warrant, and on June 25th, 1990 he died, as he had chosen to do, by lethal injection. He had refused his attorney permission to appeal. To this day speculation runs rampant as to what Simmons motive had been.

Books such as, "Zero at the Bone: The True Story of the Ronald Gene Simmons Christmas Massacre," by Paul Williams and Bryce Marshall attempt to answer the questions. But even if the motive is established - there will remain unanswered questions. How could such a family live and work in such a small town - and no one notice the signs of obvious dysfunction?

CLAY KING SMITH

Born July 25th, 1970 – executed by lethal injection in Arkansas on May 8th, 2001.

At the beginning of 1998, Clay Smith and Misty Erwin were living together at 3105 Pinto Road in Pine Bluff. On or about March 25th, 1998, Misty Erwin, 20, her cousin Shelly Sorg, 24, Sorg's two children, Taylor Sorg, 3, Sean Sorg, 5, and their friend Samantha Rhodes, 12, were murdered at that address.

Between March 23rd and 25th, 1998, Misty Erwin died from either two or three gunshot wounds; Shelly Sorg died from four gunshot wounds; Taylor Sorg died from a single gunshot wound; Sean Sorg died from two gunshot wounds; and Samantha Rhodes died from three gunshot wounds.

Just two days before on March 23rd, Corporal Calvin Terry of the Jefferson County Sheriff's Office had been dispatched to the parking lot of a store to meet Misty Erwin who had reported being battered by her boyfriend, Clay Smith. Ms. Erwin asked the officer to assist her in picking up her belongings at the apartment she shared with Smith on Pinto Road. Upon arriving at the Pinto Road residence, the officer found that Smith was present. Smith and Ms. Erwin started talking to each other, and then Ms. Erwin changed her mind and decided she would stay at the residence and not go to a women's shelter. She also decided not to press charges against Smith and signed a written statement to that effect. Corporal Terry later testified that Smith and Ms. Erwin were "getting along together fine" when he left the residence.

Andy Hoots, a patrol officer with the Jefferson County Sheriff's Office, was dispatched at 8:00 p.m. on March 25th, 1998, to a grocery store parking lot regarding a missing person's report. Once there, he met Misty Erwin's mother, Lula Erwin, who reported her daughter missing. Bobbie Erwin was also at the grocery store and reported her daughter, Shelly Sorg, and Shelly's two children, Sean and Taylor, missing. In order to make a complete report, Officer Hoots went to Pinto Road to find the street number of the residence that Lula Erwin and Bobbie Erwin described as the missing persons home. He was also looking for Misty Erwin's vehicle, which had also been reported missing. While patrolling on Pinto Road, Officer Hoots was flagged down by James Rhodes, the father of Samantha Rhodes who reported his daughter also missing.

Mr. Rhodes showed Officer Hoots the residence of Smith and Misty Erwin at 3105 Pinto Road. Officer Hoots approached the residence and knocked on the door but received no response. He then looked around the residence but was unable to see inside. While doing so, Shelly Sorg's parents came to the residence and identified their daughter's vehicle parked at the residence.

Officer Hoots left the residence in order to meet with his superior and fill him in on the situation. As he was doing so, he received another call instructing him to return to 3105 Pinto Road due to suspicious circumstances. Upon arriving back at Pinto Road at approximately 10:30 p.m., Officer Hoots was met by the owner of the property, Mark Lackey. Mr. Lackey used his key to open the door to the residence. Officer Hoots shined his flashlight inside the premises and saw blood stains on the carpet. He then leaned inside the doorway and saw blood splatters on the side of a washing machine or dryer. As he leaned inside the doorway and looked toward the back bedroom of the residence ne could see a deceased female stretched across a bed. He then backed out of the doorway, shut the door, and called his superior to report what he had found. Soon after, several police officers and investigators arrived.

One of the investigators who came to the scene was Stephen Moreau. He testified that he arrived at the crime scene on Pinto Road shortly after 11:00 p.m. He and Investigator Frank J. Moser, III, went inside the residence to check for victims needing medical attention and for possible suspects. Upon entering through the back door, they found blood on the floor just inside the door. In the west bedroom, they found a female and a small child lying on the bed, both deceased. They were identified as Samantha Rhodes and Sean Sorg. In the living room, they noticed a foot protruding from underneath a blanket covering a couch. Investigator Moreau looked under the blanket and found a deceased female. She was identified as Shelly Sorg. They also noticed the figure of a body sitting up in a recliner that was covered with a blanket. Investigator Moreau lifted a section of that blanket and found another deceased female. She was identified as Misty Erwin. After finishing their search of the house for other victims or suspects, the investigators left the residence and obtained a full search warrant.

While Investigators Moreau and Moser were in the process of preparing a search warrant, the deputy coroner arrived at the residence. Investigator Moser, Investigator Eugene Butler, and the deputy coroner went back inside the residence so the deputy coroner could pronounce death and fix the time of death. She noted the temperature in the residence and checked the bodies of each of the victims in the bedroom and the living room. It was at this point that the body of a small child was discovered under the blanket covering the couch. This was Taylor Sorg. The deputy coroner actually pronounced death at 11:41 p.m., but estimated that the victims had been dead for twenty-four to thirty-six hours.

After obtaining the search warrant, the investigators re-entered the house to videotape the crime scene, take photographs, and collect evidence. They discovered great amounts of blood around the bodies and throughout the residence. They also found twelve spent .22 calibre shell casings and two bullet fragments in the areas where the victim's bodies were found.

Clay Smith became an immediate suspect in the murders. In addition to the earlier report of a disturbance between Smith and Ms. Erwin on March 23rd, 1998, and the forensic evidence discovered at the crime scene, the police officers interviewed bystanders and neighbourhood residents. Sandra Haynes, who lived about 300 feet away from the residence on Pinto Road, testified that she looked out of her kitchen window at around 12:05 a.m. on March 25th, 1998 and saw Smith leaving the residence in a hurry.

According to Mrs. Haynes, he stopped and looked at her for about ten seconds before getting into his car and driving away. Another witness, Becky Irons, told the police that she had heard Smith threaten to kill Misty Erwin and her family if Misty left him. Ms. Irons also reported that she had seen a rifle on the couch in Misty Erwin's residence when the threat occurred. On March 26th, 1998, the prosecuting attorney filed a felony information and an arrest warrant for Clay Smith was issued.

Soon after leaving the Pinto Road residence on the 26th, the investigating officers in Jefferson County received information that Smith was at a hunting club near Star City in neighbouring Lincoln County. Accordingly, the Jefferson County officers went to Star City and met with officers from the Arkansas State Police and the Lincoln County Sheriff's Office, to discuss their plans for arresting Smith. The various officers then proceeded to the hunting club. When they arrived, Smith fled on foot through a wooded area pursued by the officers.

Smith, who was carrying a rifle, went two to three-hundred yards before he stopped running and began to walk. He then stopped walking and turned to confront the officers. At that point he was approximately fifteen yards away from them. For the next fifty-five minutes Smith engaged in a shouted conversation with the officers but refused to drop his weapon. During the standoff, he made several incriminating admissions to the killings. Finally, the confrontation ended when a state trooper shot Mr. Smith in the arm, and the officers took him into custody.

The trial began on March 17th, 1999. Smith's defence offered no witnesses on his behalf and he was found guilty and sentenced to death. He forbade them entering any appeals saying he did not want to prolong the deceased families' grief. He was executed by lethal injection on May 8th, 2001.

MARK ALLAN SMITH

Born June 27th, 1949 – sentenced to a total 500 years in 1971.

Mark Alan Smith is an American serial killer who killed at least four women in Illinois and Arkansas during the 1960s, and was sentenced to 500 years' imprisonment for three of the deaths. Smith later confessed to killing a further eight women while stationed as a soldier in West Germany, for which he was never prosecuted. Authorities believe he could well be involved in other murders, both in the USA and overseas.

Smith was born at the Illinois Masonic Hospital, to marine Charles Gilbert Smith and Delores Rechlin, who had another four children. The couple separated when Mark Smith was 2 to 3 years old, with his mother receiving primary custody. At the age of 7, she remarried, and the family moved out to McHenry, Illinois, where Smith grew up. He attended the local grade school, but anger issues and the difficulty of adjusting to a new locale resulted in his and the family's return to Chicago.

A year later, while a student at Edgebrook Public School, Smith attempted to strangle a female classmate behind the school building. One year after that, he stabbed a 6-year-old playmate with a pen knife more than 20 times. The boy managed to survive, and Mark underwent psychiatric analysis.

In 1966, Smith was enlisted in the Army during the Vietnam War and stationed in West Germany, where, in 1967, he was court-marshalled for assaulting four African-

American colleagues. After three years in the army abroad, he returned to the USA, age 21, settling in McHenry County.

On December 3rd, 1969, Smith abducted 32-year-old Obie Fay Ash of Cotter, before proceeding to rape and strangle her. After ensuring she was deceased, he repeatedly stabbed her. All of this occurred in the nearby city of Mountain Home, where Smith worked as a handyman at a TV repair shop. When she was dead, Smith tied Ash up with wire, placed her in the backseat of her own car, and drove the car near to the TV repair shop and parked it. Ash's body was discovered later the same day. Ash left behind three children. Smith later admitted to Ash's murder.

On January 27th, 1970, the 27-year-old housewife and mother of two Jean Bianchi, from McHenry, was last seen at a local laundromat on Elm Street. In the evening, she had phoned her husband to inform him that she had finished the laundry and would be home shortly, but she didn't return. Bianchi's laundry and an unfinished letter she was writing were all located at the laundromat, but no sign of her. Three days later, her body was found in a partially frozen creek near one of the town's bridges. She had been sexually assaulted and stabbed multiple times.

After chancing upon Bianchi at the laundromat Smith had forced her into his car at knifepoint, whereupon he repeatedly stabbed and raped her. He then drove out of town and dumped the body in a local stream, but as he was leaving, he saw that she was still alive and trying to climb up an embankment and escape. He quickly caught up with her, pulled her shirt over her head and continued stabbing Bianchi to the point where he could clearly hear that her lungs had collapsed. After assuring himself she was dead, Smith dumped the body into the stream again, where it was later found.

On February 27th, 1970, Smith was working at the Resin Research Laboratory, part of the Desoto Chemical Company, situated in Mount Prospect. He was left to work overtime in the late evening hours, along with 22-year-old Janice Bolyard, from Evanston. Taking the opportunity to follow her into the basement, Smith began making sexual advances which Bolyard resisted. Infuriated, he began beating her, before choking her into unconsciousness. Smith then moved her to another room, where he took off her undergarments before proceeding to rape her. After he had finished, he took her pantyhose and wrapped it around her neck, strangling her to death. She was discovered the next day, after she'd been reported missing by her fiancé.

On May 27th, 1970, 17-year-old Jean Ann Lingenfelter, an honours student at McHenry's local high school who had previously dated with Mark Smith at the school prom, left her home so she could study at a friend's house as she was only a week away from graduation. After two hours, she left the house so she could meet Smith, and was last seen entering his vehicle. After she did not return home, her parents reported her missing. The next day, her naked body was found by a young couple on a beach at Lakeland Park. Her body showed signs of rape, severe beating and strangulation, as well as sexual assault of her vagina and rectum.

Smith admitted that he raped and strangled Lingenfelter, later inserting a beer bottle in both her vagina and rectum after she had died. He then put the lifeless body in the trunk of his car, and dumped it at McCollum Lake.

Aside from these murders, Smith himself confessed to killing between three and eight women in West Germany during his army enlistment, which he later recanted to just two. German authorities never prosecuted him for these alleged killings, despite his confessions being investigated and found to be credible.

The prosecutors at his trial alleged that his victim count likely exceeds 20 in number, but because his crimes covered a two-year period over a large geographic area, they were largely ignored and not connected. Authorities have questioned him regarding murders in South Vietnam, South Korea, five other U.S.A states and in Washington D.C, as well as the still unsolved Kenilworth 1966 murder of 21-year-old Valerie Percy, daughter of businessman and Republican politician Charles H Percy.

The murders of Bianchi and Lingenfelter had shocked the population of McHenry, and large amounts of people had joined in the search for the killer, one of them being Mark Alan Smith himself. He was arrested and charged with murder, after he himself discovered Lingenfelter's body "by accident", but, the police thought, with surprising accuracy. He was interviewed shortly after his arrest and displayed cold-blooded indifference towards the victim.

He later confessed to the two killings, as well as those of Ash and Bolyard. He was sentenced to 500 years' imprisonment for the Illinois murders in 1971. He dodged the death penalty, as there was a moratorium of it at the time.

On April 27th, 1977, Smith was caught trying to escape from the Pontiac Correctional Centre through the boiler room, to which he later pleaded guilty and was given another 18 years. While serving his time, Smith's defence attorney, Harold C. McKenney, aided by Jon K. Hahn, helped Smith co-author a book, titled "Legally Sane", in which Smith described his life and crime spree in vivid detail, where he also admits to the killings in Germany.

Every 3 years, he has a mandatory hearing for parole, but he claims to know that being released is unlikely. He now claims, at 75 years old, to be a changed man who can reintegrate into society, having chosen a new identity for himself—Remington Steele. Even if he was to be released, he would have to be transferred to Arkansas, where he will serve a life sentence for the killing of Obie Fay Ash. At the time of writing Smith currently remains incarcerated at Pontiac, where he earns an income through selling oil paintings to guards, and is currently studying for his third college degree.

RICHARD WAYNE SNELL

Born 1931 – executed by lethal injection in Arkansas April 19th, 1995.

Richard Wayne Snell was a member of a number of white supremacy groups, including The Covenant, The Sword, and the Arm of The Lord, which was founded in 1971 in Elijah, Missouri, by polygamist James Ellison. He was also reported to be a member of the Aryan Nation. In addition, there are unsubstantiated reports connecting Snell to Oklahoma City bomber Timothy McVeigh who's act of domestic terrorism occurred only hours before Snell's execution for two murders he had committed in the 1980s.

Snell was born in Iowa on May 21st, 1930, to Charles Edwin Snell and Mary Jane Snell. His father was a pastor of the Church of Nazarene, and Snell himself trained in the ministry but did not pursue it. Not much is known about his youth, but he became an active participant in a number of extreme right-wing organizations. His involvement appears to have stemmed from a series of interactions Snell had with governmental agencies, with each encounter seemingly fuelling his intense anti-government hatred. One of his grievances was with the Internal Revenue Service (IRS), and it was later reported that in 1983, in anger, he had expressed a desire to blow up the Oklahoma City Federal Building as revenge for IRS agents having previously raided his home.

At one point, Snell was involved in a project in which he filmed planes that landed at the Mena Intermountain Municipal Airport in Mena, Polk County. Snell apparently believed that the CIA was using the airport to smuggle drugs and thought that the local and state political forces were involved in covering up the operation. In fairness, Mena attracted a great deal of national and international attention in the 1980s and 1990s due to its role in an immense drug-smuggling operation and the Iran-Contra Scandal, with the airport at the centre of those activities. On another occasion, he claimed that an Arkansas State trooper, a member of the governor's security detail, had beaten Snell's wife, Mary Jo, in an attempt to get her to reveal where Snell was keeping the film footage that he had compiled.

Much of his activity stemmed from his association with the Covenant, the Sword, and the Arm of the Lord, a paramilitary organization headquartered in the hill country of northern Arkansas. His association with the group led to his being indicted in the late 1980s, along with a dozen other white supremacists, for conspiring to overthrow the government. While he was ultimately acquitted in the 1988 trial, this incident only added to his anti-government rage. Despite his association with various radical right organizations, Snell appeared to be something of an independent operator. While he was recognized as a member of the CSA, he primarily used it as a base of operations for his own autonomous anti-government activities. He was also said to be a member of the Aryan Nation and spent much time in Elohim City, a private gated community located in Oklahoma and founded by members of the CSA.

On June 30th, 1984, he fled across state lines into Oklahoma after killing Arkansas State Trooper Louis Bryant, an African-American man. A truck driver who had witnessed the shooting followed Snell and contacted the Broken Bow, Oklahoma, police department, which set up a roadblock and had a gun battle with Snell who was wounded and captured. He was brought back to Arkansas for trial.

Following the arrest, a gun connected to an earlier murder of Texarkana, Mille County pawnshop owner William Stumpp, whom Snell wrongly believed to be Jewish, was found in his car.

After a trial that began in late October of 1984, Snell was convicted of the murder of Trooper Bryant, and a death sentence was handed down on November 1st. That same day, prosecutors charged him with the murder of Stumpp. That trial took place the following August and also resulted in a conviction for murder. Snell was again given the death penalty. Whilst he never denied the accusations of murder, he nevertheless undertook what became a decade-long effort to overturn the convictions and avoid the death penalty.

An appeal in the Stumpp case was heard by the Arkansas Supreme Court, which upheld the conviction and the accompanying sentence. His petition for a writ of habeas corpus was denied by the district court, and that ruling was upheld by Eighth Circuit Court of Appeals in January 1994. At a final appearance before the Clemency Board shortly before his execution, Snell showed no remorse and said he would probably kill Trooper Bryant again if the same circumstances were to present themselves.

In addition to the murders for which Snell was convicted, he was also at the centre of rumours relating to Timothy McVeigh and the Oklahoma City bombings of April 19th, 1995, the same day that Snell was executed. At McVeigh's trial, his defence attorney, in an effort to cast blame beyond McVeigh and his fellow conspirator, tried to introduce a government memo that called Snell "the driving force" behind a plot that had surfaced in 1983, twelve years earlier, to bomb the same Oklahoma City federal building. There were also reports that, in the days before the Oklahoma City bombing, Snell had predicted that there would be a bombing or explosion on the day of his execution. As he awaited his own execution and watched the news reports of the Oklahoma City bombings, officials who were monitoring his actions prior to the execution said that, while he seemed to smile at the news, he had also noted that it was the second anniversary of the government's explosive showdown with the Branch Davidians in Waco, Texas, an event that had done much to energize the extreme right wing of the political spectrum, which saw it as the embodiment of the excessive governmental power that they deplored.

Richard Snell was executed on April 19th, 1995. As he was taken to his execution, the ever-defiant Snell was reported to have offered a parting bit of advice to Governor Jim Guy Tucker and his "cronies." to "Look over your shoulder, justice is coming."

JOHN EDWARD SWINDLER

Born 1944 – executed by electrocution in Arkansas on June 18th, 1990

John Edward Swindler was a violent criminal who was executed on June 18th, 1990, for the 1976 murder of Fort Smith, Sebastian County, patrolman Randy Basnett. He was the first Arkansas death row inmate executed following reinstatement of the death penalty in 1977. The last execution before Swindler had been in 1964. He was the last Arkansas inmate to be executed in the electric chair.

Having been in many penal institutions since the age of fifteen, Swindler was released from the United States Prison at Leavenworth, Kansas, on September 17th, 1976. He returned to his home state of South Carolina, where a former cellmate provided him with a gun. He began a crime spree that included abductions; an attempted abduction; the shooting and killing of three people; the tying up of an elderly couple whom he robbed of guns, ammunition, and a vehicle; and a service station robbery that left the attendant paralyzed after being shot.

Angry about his perceived mistreatment at Leavenworth, Swindler planned to return to Kansas, kill as many citizens as he could, and then shoot as many police officers as possible. Unable to read the road signs, Swindler was lost much of the time on the road and had to often ask for directions. On September 24th, 1976, he took a wrong turn that brought him into Fort Smith.

Stopping at the Road Runner convenience store and service station on Kelley Highway, just off Interstate 540, Swindler entered the store where Patrolman Basnett was visiting with the owner. Basnett recognized the stolen vehicle and Swindler from a national bulletin issued by the FBI earlier that day. Leaving the store after receiving directions to Kansas, Swindler inspected the car's engine while Basnett proceeded to his patrol car, radioed for backup, and pulled his car behind the stolen vehicle to block it. Swindler shut the hood and got into the car as Basnett approached the car and spoke with him. A witness later testified that from the seated position in the car, Swindler suddenly brought up a pistol and fired it, striking Basnett twice.

Although mortally wounded, Basnett was able to fire his gun at the vehicle, resulting in superficial wounds for Swindler who rammed his car into the police vehicle to clear the way out. He then fled east on Kelley Highway. Arkansas State Police from the Troop Headquarters just across Kelley Highway followed Swindler and were backed up by responding Fort Smith officers. They found Swindler's car abandoned in a wooded area near the Arkansas River, and as police moved in, Swindler walked out of the woods and surrendered. Basnett was pronounced dead on arrival at Spark's Memorial Medical Centre.

Swindler was treated for his wounds and placed in the Sebastian County jail. A public defender was appointed, and a plea of not guilty was entered to a charge of murder. Swindler was held without bond. The public defender requested a psychiatric evaluation of Swindler at the Arkansas State Hospital in Little Rock, Pulaski County that declared him free of psychosis and competent to stand trial, and so he was returned to the Sebastian County jail.

Following a two-day hearing, the circuit judge denied Swindler's request for a change of venue. Dissatisfied with his attorneys, Swindler asked the circuit court and later the federal district court to appoint new counsel. The requests were denied, and the case proceeded to trial in February 1977. Swindler argued that he had acted in self-defence, saying that he had "heard a gun cock real close" and was hit twice by bullets and that he then returned fire before he realized the individual was a police officer. He also claimed that he "was pretty well high on vodka when it happened." The Sebastian County jury found him guilty of capital felony murder after deliberating for forty-five minutes, sentencing him to death in the electric chair.

Swindler appealed, and the Arkansas Supreme Court, in 1978, reversed and remanded the case, holding that a change of venue was necessary in such a case and that three of the jurors should have been disqualified due to the pre-trial publicity they admitted to having seen.

An October 1978 a re-trial in Waldron, Scott County, produced an identical jury verdict of guilty and the penalty of death. On appeal a second time, the Arkansas Supreme Court, in 1979, affirmed the verdict and sentence. A 1981 appeal arguing inadequacy of legal counsel was rejected by the Arkansas Supreme Court. The U.S. Supreme Court declined to hear the appeal.

Swindler began the first of two habeas corpus appeals in August 1988. His attorneys argued that mental health and other mitigating factors should have been considered at trial. His arguments were rejected by U.S. District Judge Henry Woods. The Eighth Circuit Court of Appeals upheld the judge's decision, and the U.S. Supreme Court declined to hear the case. With appeals exhausted, the stay of execution was lifted, and Governor Bill Clinton refused clemency and signed the proclamation for Swindler's execution to take place on June 18th, 1990.

Whilst in prison Swindler had developed friendships with anti–death penalty activists and clergy, three of whom spoke on his behalf before the parole board in a late bid for executive clemency, asking that his sentence be changed to life without parole. Speaking against clemency were the family of Basnett, a former guard at the prison, and a prosecutor. The board voted 5–0 to recommend denial of clemency. Governor Clinton followed that recommendation.

In a second habeas corpus appeal in June 1990, Swindler argued erroneous jury selection and instructions, petitioning for a stay of execution. The federal district court denied the stay, as did the Eighth Circuit Court of Appeals.

As the appeal moved to the U.S. Supreme Court, preparations for his execution proceeded. Swindler had been sentenced to die in the electric chair. In 1983, however, Arkansas changed the method of execution from electric chair to lethal injection. Given the choice, Swindler declined to choose. Absent a choice, authorities upheld the original sentence of electrocution.

In the early morning hours of June 15th, 1990, Swindler was moved from death row at the Varner Unit to a small cell near the death chamber at Cummins Unit. There, he was allowed to direct the final disposition of his items, give instructions for the final disposition of his remains, and choose a last meal.

The next day, the U.S. Supreme Court, with Justices William J. Brennen and Thurgood Marshall dissenting, denied the request for a stay of execution. Swindler's attorneys acknowledged that there was no basis for further appeal.

On the day of the execution, June 18th, 1990, visitors were limited to Swindler's religious advisor and his attorney.

Swindler was led to the death chamber and to Arkansas's second electric chair. The large oak chair was built in 1976 and replaced the one built in 1913 that had been used through 1964. Swindler would be the first and last inmate to be executed in the new chair.

At 9:02 p.m. June 18th, 1990, Swindler, age 46, became the first person to be executed in Arkansas in twenty-six years. He was pronounced dead by the Lincoln County Coroner a few minutes later. He is buried in Calvary Cemetery, Pulaski County, Arkansas.

BILLY THESSING

Born September 11th, 1968 - sentenced to death September 20th, 2004.

On February 17th, 2003, Susan Basinger Sweet went to the home of her mother, Mattie Basinger, a sixty-seven year old cancer survivor and noticed that Ms. Basinger's car was not there. She sent her son, Jeremiah, into the house first, but Susan and her children followed and found Ms. Basinger dead. They immediately went back outside and called the Little Rock Police Department.

Takeisha Gilbert, a patrol officer for the department, was the first officer to arrive at the scene. She observed blood throughout the house and found Ms. Basinger's body in the bedroom. The autopsy later revealed that Ms. Basinger had a total of six stab and cutting wounds on multiple parts of her body. She also received blunt force wounds to her head.

Two of the stab wounds were in her cheek region, which caused bleeding inside her mouth. The bleeding in her mouth had caused her to aspirate blood into her trachea that subsequently went into her lungs. The medical examiner testified at trial that Ms. Basinger was alive when she received all these injuries. He also concluded Ms. Basinger was alive and breathing in her own blood for ten to fifteen minutes before a blunt force trauma to her head caused her death.

On February17th, 2003, Pam McNew went to the Benton Police Department to talk to police officers after seeing a television news report about Ms. Basinger's murder. She testified later, at trial, that Billy Thessing, a friend of her's since childhood, came to her house late on the evening of February 11th, 2003.

She saw him when she returned from a convenience store. He was burning trash in her front yard. They both went into her house, and he told her that he had killed someone earlier that evening. He then went back outside and brought in some groceries, a television set, vitamins, unfilled prescription slips, and a large Bible. Ms. McNew also told the authorities that the car he drove to her house was the car that belonged to Ms. Basinger. She later found Ms. Basinger's wheelchair in her shed. Police officers also found silverware and credit cards on the premises which were taken from Ms. Basinger.

Ms. McNew further stated that Thessing had tried to convince her fiancé, who was also at her house, to go with him to burn down Ms. Basinger's home so that it would make the murder look like an accident. At the ensuing trial, Ms. McNew testified that she, Thessing, and her fiancé had used crack cocaine together that night.

Although Ms. McNew did not believe Thessing at first, she later ordered him to leave her house, because she had a child and because she did not want to get in trouble herself for harbouring him. She stated that Thessing left in Ms. Basinger's car. After her visit to the police station officers came and recovered all the things Thessing had left at her home. Ms. McNew later received a $400 reward for going to the police.

Later on February 17th, 2003, Thessing wrecked Ms. Basinger's car and was arrested by a Benton police officer for public intoxication. Inside Ms. Basinger's car, police officers found a pair of boots with Ms. Basinger's blood on them which were matched to bloody boot prints found at Ms.

Basinger's house. Additionally, police investigators found Thessing's fingerprints in Ms. Basinger's home.

On April 16th, 2003, the prosecuting attorney filed a four-count information against Thessing, charging him with capital murder, residential burglary, and theft by receiving property valued in excess of $2500.00. The information further charged Thessing with misdemeanour theft by receiving property valued at less than $500.00. The information added that Thessing was a habitual offender with four or more prior felony convictions.

Before trial, Thessing moved for an order that he was incompetent to stand trial. He was later judged as competent to stand trial at a pre-trial hearing. He was tried and convicted of all four charges against him and was sentenced to death for the capital murder charge.

Thessing's appeals continue at the time of writing.

MICKEY DAVID THOMAS

Born September 25th, 1974 – sentenced to death in Arkansas on September 28th, 2005.

On June 14th, 2005, DeQueen Police found the bodies of two women at Cornerstone Monument Company after receiving a call about a possible break in at the property.

Mona Shelton, the owner of the company, had been beaten and shot once in the head. Donna Cary, a customer, had been shot once in the head at close range. Police received a witness report of a black male with a white bag walking away from the front of Cornerstone Monument Company and getting into a pewter or copper-coloured Ford Mustang with an Oklahoma license plate. Police broadcast this description to area law enforcement officers, and at 11:27 a.m., Trooper Jamie Gravier of the Arkansas State Police spotted the Mustang travelling west near the Oklahoma-Arkansas border. Gravier attempted to stop the vehicle, and a high-speed chase ensued into Broken Bow, Oklahoma.

Oklahoma police ultimately located the vehicle parked behind the Broken Bow residence of Hazel Thomas, Mickey Thomas's mother, but the driver had already left the area. That same afternoon, police received a report that a black male with a gun had just stolen a Broken Bow resident's Mercury Cougar. The Oklahoma authorities spotted the vehicle, and they were able to stop it after a chase and arrest Thomas.

He was extradited to Arkansas and was charged in Sevier County with two counts of capital murder for the deaths of Mona Shelton and Donna Cary. The case was transferred to Pike County where he was convicted of the two counts of capital murder and was given a sentence of death for each one.

It became known at his trial that Thomas was wanted in Oklahoma for the murder of Geraldine Jones who he had killed as she held a garage sale at her property and he had a criminal history of kidnapping and robbery convictions only having been released after a nine year prison sentence a year before the Cornerstone Monument Company killings.

At the time of writing Thomas is being held in a 'supermax' prison in Varner, Arkansas as his appeals roll on.

EARL VAN DENTON

Born 1949 – executed by lethal injection in Arkansas January 8th, 1997.
See under PAUL RUIZ

KIRT DOUGLAS WAINWRIGHT

Born 1966 – executed by lethal injection in Arkansas on January 8th, 1997.

Kirt Wainwright was convicted of killing Barbara Smith, an attendant at the Best Stop convenience store in Prescott, Arkansas. Ms. Smith was shot during a robbery on July 29th, 1988. Although no one saw the actual murder, witnesses saw Wainwright run out of the store after the robbery and jump into a pink Cadillac. Police were given the description and a short time later saw the pink Cadillac and pulled it over. Andrew Woods was driving the car and Dennis Leeper was riding in the front seat. Wainwright was in the back seat with a Best Stop money bag containing cash and a gun. The State charged all three men with capital murder.

At Wainwright's trial, the State presented evidence that Wainwright was the person who went into the Best Stop alone and committed the robbery and murder while Leeper and Woods waited in the car. Wainwright argued Leeper was the triggerman. After hearing the evidence, an Arkansas jury convicted Wainwright of capital felony murder. At the conclusion of the penalty phase, the trial court submitted special verdict forms to the jury. On these forms, the jury unanimously found three aggravating circumstances existed at the time of the murder: Wainwright had previously committed another felony involving a threat of violence to another person, the murder was committed to avoid or prevent arrest, and the murder was committed for pecuniary gain. The jury also unanimously found two mitigating circumstances: Wainwright had no history of homicide before the murder of Ms. Smith, and Wainwright did not resist when arrested for murdering her. The jury then unanimously found the aggravating circumstances outweighed any mitigating circumstances and justified a sentence of death.

Several witnesses who arrived at the scene during or just after the murder took place testified they saw a single black man run out of the Best Stop. A witness testified the man was wearing red and white flowered shorts, and another testified he jumped into a pink Cadillac that sped away. A young man who knew Wainwright through family connections testified he was walking by the Best Stop at the time of the murder and saw Wainwright run out of the store. The young man was sure the fleeing man was Kirt Wainwright because he saw Wainwright's face. Moments later, he saw a pink Cadillac speed by him. The young man testified he saw Wainwright in the back seat and two other people in the car.

When police stopped the pink Cadillac soon after the murder, Leeper and Woods were in the front, and Wainwright was in the back seat with the Best Stop money bag and a gun. Ballistics tests revealed the gun could have been the one used to kill Ms. Smith. Wainwright was wearing red and white flowered shorts when apprehended and the shorts were later identified as the ones the witness had seen on the man running from inside the Best Stop. Neither Leeper nor Woods was wearing red shorts.

Wainwright's appeals ran out in 1996 and he was executed by lethal injection on January 8th. 1997. Both Leeper and Woods were found guilty of assisting a felonious crime and received life sentences.

January 8th, 1997 was a triple execution day in Arkansas with Wainwright, Paul Ruiz and Earl Van Denton being executed one after the other from 7pm.

JONAS HOTEN WHITMORE

On the afternoon of August 14th, 1986, the body of sixty-two-year-old Essie Mae Black was found in the bedroom of her home in Mount Ida, Arkansas, lying between two beds. She had been stabbed at least ten times in her front and back, her throat had been cut, and an X had been carved into the right side of her face.

$150 was missing from Mrs. Black's purse which was found with its contents spilled out on a bed next to the body and $126 was missing from a kitchen drawer. A knife and clothing belonging to Jonas Whitmore were found in a wooded area close by stained with blood of the same type as Mrs. Black. The labels had been removed from the clothes but were found in the same general area.

Jonas Whitmore was arrested on September 23rd, 1986, in Roundup, Montana and returned to Arkansas where, after a change of venue to Scott County, he was tried on a charge of the capital murder of Mrs Black. At his trial, Whitmore testified that on August 14th, 1986, he was in Mount Ida looking for property to rent or buy and that he stopped at the home of Mrs. Black to ask her if she knew of any cheap trailer houses or property to rent or buy in the area. Not knowing of anything available off hand, Mrs. Black invited Whitmore inside her home to see if she could be of any help by calling a friend. Once inside, Mrs. Black sat down at a kitchen table and asked Whitmore to hand her a purse that was sitting on what he described as a "buffet counter top or china closet or something that looked like an old antique". Whitmore handed Mrs. Black the purse and a cheque book that had fallen out, and asked permission to use the bathroom. When he emerged from the bathroom, Mrs.

Black was in the hallway talking on the telephone in an attempt to provide him with the information he was seeking. Whitmore testified at his later trial that Mrs. Black mentioned a newspaper that listed property for sale and rent, which he had noticed lying on the floor in the bedroom, and that when he bent down to pick it up, he experienced a "flashback" of his mother and aunt who he claims abused him as a child. Exactly what happened next is not clear, but Whitmore remembers his hand was moving "up and down" as he was telling Mrs. Black "don't mom, don't," and remembers later walking out to his car with blood all over him. He also testified that when he left the residence, Mrs. Black was sitting on the bed "whimpering".

Whitmore drove down the highway and pulled off into a wooded area where he removed the labels from his clothes and then discarded the clothes behind a tree because they were bloody. He washed his hands and the knife he was carrying but threw the knife away when he was unable to remove all the blood. He later threw his shoes away, and drove into the town of Hot Springs, Arkansas, where he purchased a "fancy card" for his wife and a carton of cigarettes with a one-hundred-dollar bill. He later purchased gas with another one-hundred-dollar bill.

Whitmore was picked out of a photo line-up by Clara Stanley, a neighbour of Mrs Black. Whitmore had stopped at Mrs Stanley's house and talked to her over her fence about renting a trailer in the area before going onto Mrs Black's home.

Whitmore was convicted of capital murder by a jury in the Scott County, Arkansas, Circuit Court and, following the penalty phase of his trial, sentenced to death by lethal injection. The Arkansas Supreme Court affirmed his conviction and sentence on direct appeal.

Jonas Whitmore was executed by lethal injection in Arkansas on May 11th, 1994 aged 50.

ALAN WILLET

Born 1947 – executed by lethal injection September 8th, 1999

Ian Willett was an unemployed 46 year old Arkansas man living with his family in a trailer park. He divorced his wife in 1992, and she moved to California. Willet was left alone with their 3 children, 17 year old Ruby, 13 year old Eric, 8 year old John, and his intellectually disabled brother, 43 year Roger, to take care of.

Willett neglected his children and brother alike. Visitors to the trailer home described their living conditions as a "putrid squalor." He had child services call on him numerous times, including a pastor that visited the home to invite them to his church, and the children's teachers noticed that their clothes looked very dirty and their bodies seemed a little too thin. However, the social workers didn't find anything wrong in their investigations, and allowed the Willett family situation to continue on unchallenged.

It didn't take long for tensions in the family to escalate beyond the boiling point. On September 14th, 1993, Willett assaulted his children and brother with an eight pound iron window weight. Roger and Eric were killed in the attack. Ruby shielded John with her own body, and dragged him and herself to the safety of a neighbour's house. She hid him under a bush until she was able to wave their neighbour down as he returned from work. Both had suffered serious injuries, but they managed to survive.

When the police arrived at the scene, Willett had already slit his own throat and wrists, locked himself in the bathroom, and threatened to shoot himself with his gun.

Despite his initial resistance, the officers were able to subdue and arrest him. In the following trial, Willett was sentenced to death for the murders of his son and brother.

At first, Willett tried appealing his sentence but at each appeal the sentence was affirmed. After a few years of incarceration he changed his mind, and volunteered for the execution telling staff he wanted to die for what he had done. He was put to death on September 8th, 1999 by lethal injection alongside another convicted murderer, Mark Gardner.

ARKANSAS LADIES

LAVINIA VENY BURNETT (nee SHARP)

Born 1790 – hanged with her husband Crawford Burnett November 8th, 1845.

Although a bit before the time span of this book Sharp is included here because she was the first woman to be executed in the state of Arkansas.

The following story was printed in a Washington County, Arkansas Newspaper about 1950, some parts are illegible, it reads as follows:
'The early history of Washington County was not, for a frontier country, particularly bloody. But the period from 1829 until well up toward the turn of the century was a time when most men went armed and violence was accepted as a natural part of frontier life.

And Northwest Arkansas was, even many years after the founding of Washington County, a frontier. To the west was the Indian Territory, noted as home territory for outlaws and cut-throats. The Ozark Mountains served as home to many men who had, all their lives, depended on their weapons for security.

By 1845, Fayetteville, the county seat, had known several murder trials - mostly ending in acquittals - but none of the defendants has been executed.

THREE ARE HANGED

But in the fall and winter of 1845 - 105 years ago this winter - a man, his wife, and their son were hanged in Fayetteville for the murder of a recluse who had lived near Fayetteville. Many people believed the trio not guilty, but a daughter of the older suspects gave testimony which clinched the case for the state and ended in a death verdict for the couple and their son.

During the late summer of 1845, a bachelor named Jonathan Selby was murdered at his home several miles outside of Fayetteville. The theory was that Selby had been killed for a large sum of money he supposedly kept hidden in his home. Selby was possibly the first, but far from the last, Washington County resident to be slain for money supposedly hoarded under a mattress or in the attic.

Why suspicion fell on Crawford Burnett, his wife, Mrs. Lavinia Burnett and their son John is not known. The parents were arrested and jailed but the son John had left for Missouri and could not be found.

Following the arrests the Burnetts' 15 year old daughter, Minerva, reported that the murder had been planned by her mother and father, and carried out by her absent brother. Some of the county's most capable and respected attorneys doubted the child's story, but the jury believed it.

Mr. and Mrs. Burnett were tried at a special term of Circuit Court in October 1845. Interest in the case ran high. In an area where the population was still small, most people knew either the victim or his alleged slayers and opinion was divided.

The special term opened Friday October 3rd with Circuit Judge Gibson G. Sneed, presiding Sheriff Elijah OBrian was ordered to summon 38 men for a Grand Jury. The Grand Jury was empanelled without waste of time, instructed by the prosecuting attorney, A.H. Greenwood and retired to deliberate.

Before noon, Thomas Wilson, foreman of the Grand Jury, reported that the jurors had indicted Crawford and Lavinia Burnett on a charge of murder in the death of Selby.

The following day, Saturday, October 4th, both defendants pleaded not guilty and asked for a trial by jury. Judge Sneed ordered the sheriff to secure a jury panel and released Minerva Burnett, the daughter until Monday, October 6th under a $100 bond. A second witness, Hardin Sharp was freed under a similar bond.

Court convened Monday morning and the Burnett's attorney Charles G. Baylor asked to be relieved of his duties. Judge Sneed complied with the request and appointed Isaac Stinin and James Neil as defence attorneys. A third Fayetteville lawyer, Isaac Murphy later to serve as governor of Arkansas, volunteered to aid the defence.

Burnett and his wife were tried separately. On Wednesday a jury was assembled to hear the case against Crawford Burnett. The testimony given by his daughter Minerva... (illegible) that the jury had found Burnett guilty of first degree murder.

The following day, Lavinia Burnett went on trial for her life. His attorneys attempted to ... (the testimony of Hardin Sharp illegible)...Nothing is now known of Sharps testimony... Again Minerva Burnett testified

224

that she had heard her parents plotting the death of Selby with her brother John. As in the previous trial the jury deliberated briefly before returning a guilty verdict.

On Tuesday, October 10th, Judge Sneed pronounced sentence on the two defendants, ordering them taken to the common gallows and hanged by the neck until dead. On Saturday, November 8th, both Burnett and his wife were hanged from a gallows where the National Cemetery is now located.

The court had ordered that the sentence be carried out between 12 oclock noon and 3 p.m. A large crowd had gathered some time before the executions and it appears that almost every person in the county who was able to reach Fayetteville that day was on hand by the time of the executions.

A few days after the execution of his parents, John Burnett was arrested in Missouri and returned to Fayetteville for trial. The youth, his exact age is unknown, was promptly tried in Circuit Court before Judge Sneed, found guilty and sentenced to death.

Young Burnett was indicted by a Grand Jury December 1st and efforts to select a jury began the following day. Although no record of the proceedings was kept in those days, the bare record of court proceedings indicates that Burnett's attorneys put up a fight. The lawyers appear to have believed in the innocence of their client, but the testimony of the sister convinced the jury that Burnett was guilty and on December 26th, the day after Christmas, John Burnett was led to the gallows where his parents had died and hanged by the neck until dead.

The testimony of the case was reviewed by many well-known and highly influential attorneys after the death of the three Burnetts and it was the general consensus that the daughter Minerva lied about her parents and brother out of some sort of revenge. Nothing is recorded as to what happened to her.'

DOLORES JEAN EGGERT

Born August 29th, 1959 - sentenced to 30 years in prison on August 15th, 2010

Pauline Devore was 70 when she disappeared in June 2007. Her husband Bob Devore claimed to have returned home from a business trip to find his wife missing and his house burglarized. Several thousand dollars and 14 guns were missing. It was two years later that the police were able to gather enough evidence to arrest Dolores Eggert, Pauline Devore's daughter from a previous marriage, and charge her with the murder of her mother.

From the start of the investigation the police had suspicions that Pauline Devore's disappearance was not what it seemed. Two bullet holes in a wall inside the house did not fit the crime. If Pauline had been shot during a robbery where was the blood? Her husband, Bob Devore, was seemingly not at all upset and didn't pester the police for information on what was happening in their search for his disappearing wife, which was most unusual for the husband of a missing person. And then when it came out that he had been having a sexual relationship with Dolores Rggert the alarm bells rang.

But it wasn't until 2 years later that things ramped up when a witness came forward. Monica Bautista told police in 2009 that she helped Eggert plan the murder and lure Pauline to a location on the Devore's large farm, shoot her and burn the body. Remnants from the fire were taken to a river and thrown in. The police searched the place where Bautista said the fire had been and gathered miniscule fragments of burnt bone and two dental crowns that were identified as Pauline Devore's by dental records.

The police brought on board three other friends of Eggert who wore wires and recorded phone calls that had Eggert admitting to the murder. A male friend came forward to tell the police that Eggert had given him an amount of guns to look after shortly after Pauline's disappearance saying she didn't like them in the house. Guns registered to Bob Devore that he had said were stolen in the robbery.

When police went to arrest Eggert she saw them arrive and locked herself in the bathroom and swallowed an amount of sleeping pills. It wasn't enough and first responders were able to induce vomiting and clear her stomach.

At trial Eggert, 49, pleaded guilty to first degree murder to avoid the death sentence and was sentenced to thirty years without parole at the Arkansas Department of Correction. Police believe the murder was carried out because Pauline had discovered Eggert had stolen and used a credit card belonging to her and also had become aware of her daughter's affair with her husband and was about to bring theft charges which could have resulted in a prison sentence for Eggert.

Bob Devore, who had helped cover up the murder was sentenced to ten years and a $15,000 fine for hindering the apprehension and prosecution of a felon.

Monica Bautista was not charged.

DOROTHY JEAN MATAJKE

Born 1930 – sentenced to life in prison plus 60 years in Arkansas 1987.

Dorothy Matajke began working as a nurse's aide and professional companion for the elderly in the 1970s in Iowa. So it came as no surprise to anyone when several of her aged and ill patients died, and there were no suggestions of foul play except where her client's money was concerned which led to police investigating into the financial dealings of her deceased patients.

In 1973 the investigations led to Matajke being convicted of fraud and sentenced to five years in prison. She escaped in February 1974 and remained at large until 1980, when she was recaptured and returned to finish out her sentence. Despite the prison break, she was given parole in 1983, serving less than the original five years. Upon release, Matajke moved to Little Rock and picked up with her old profession as a live-in nurse's aide.

On March 24th, 1985, she moved in with Paul Kinsey, 72, and his wife Opal, age 71. When Opal died on April 5th that year, the cause was listed as a recently-discovered cancer. Paul Kinsey's health began deteriorating rapidly after his wife's death, but relatives attributed his lapse to grief and loneliness.

On September 9th, 1986, Matajke acquired a new client, Marion Doyle aged 74. Another cancer patient, Doyle survived nine days of nursing by Matajke, but her death was not ascribed to cancer.

Rather, a police report suggested that the woman had committed suicide. A routine inventory, made by the executor of Doyle's estate, discovered several cheques made out to Dorothy Matajke, totalling almost $4,000.

The executor thought that there was something curious about Doyle's signature on the cheques, it didn't match her signature on other official papers. The police were informed of his suspicion and her body was exhumed for re-examination. Tissue samples showed sufficient content of arsenic to cause a fatal overdose. Meanwhile, Paul Kinsey's health continued to decline.

The old man stubbornly refused to eat or take his medication, telling relatives that every meal or dose prepared by his nurse left him feeling deathly ill. Kinsey ordered Matajke out of his house on October 28th, and three days later he was hospitalized in critical condition.

Dorothy Matajke managed to lie her way past relatives and doctors to visit her ex-patient in the emergency room, and she was still sat by his side when detectives, called by the hospital staff, arrived to arrest her. Initially, the "nurse" was charged with forgery and theft for looting Marion Doyle's bank account. Subsequent charges included felony possession of a firearm, and additional counts of forgery relating to cheques written on Paul Kinsey's account.

A search of Matajke's home yielded bottles of drugs and tranquilizers, along with three bottles of arsenic-based ant poison, and more serious charges were added to her charge sheet. On November 24th, she was accused of first-degree murder in the death of Marion Doyle and first-degree battery in the non-fatal poisoning of Paul Kinsey.

Opal Kinsey's body was exhumed December 5th, with the results of laboratory tests kept secret pending disposition of the standing charges. After Paul Kinsey died, on February

10th, 1987, assault charges were replaced with another count of first-degree murder.

In June 1987, Matajke was convicted of Paul Kinsey's murder and sentenced to life. Two months later, in a negotiated guilty plea bargain to avoid execution, she received another term of 60 years for killing Marion Doyle.

New investigations were scheduled into the deaths of several patients "cared for" by Matajke when in Iowa. Nothing is known of these and possibly they were left on the file seeing that Matajke will already spend her whole life in prison.

ELEAZAR PAULA MENDEZ

Born 1962 – sentenced to life in prison without parole on May 18th, 2007 after pleading guilty to murdering her three children.

Police rushed to the home of Eleazar Mendez, 44, in south west Arkansas on January 28th, 2006, after taking a call from her husband working in New York that she had phoned him to say she was going to kill their three children and herself after he had told her a few days before that he wanted a divorce.

At the house officers found the bodies of the three children, twins aged 5 and their 8 year old brother laying side by side on a bed and their mother collapsed with arsenic poisoning taken by dissolving ant poison in warm water. She had not taken sufficient to kill herself and recovered in hospital to face three murder charges.

Eleazar pleaded guilty to three counts of capital murder thus avoiding the death penalty and was sentenced to life in prison without parole on May 18th, 2007.

CHRISTINA MARIE RIGGS

Born September 2nd, 1971- executed by lethal injection in Arkansas on May 2nd 2000.

On November 4th, 1997, Riggs obtained the anti-depressant Elavil from her pharmacist together with the painkiller morphine and the toxic chemical potassium chloride from the hospital where she worked.

The heart-stopping potassium chloride is one of the drugs used in the lethal cocktail injected into condemned inmates being executed.

Riggs gave her two children a small amount of Elavil to put them to sleep. Then she placed each of the children in their beds.

About 10 p.m., she injected 5 year old Justin with undiluted potassium chloride. But unless it is diluted, the drug causes burning and pain. Justin woke in pain and cried out in terror. Riggs then smothered the boy with a pillow.

Moving to her 2 year old daughter Shelby, Riggs discarded the potassium chloride injection because of the pain it had caused Justin and suffocated Shelby with a pillow.

Riggs then placed the children side-by-side on her bed and covered them with a blanket. She wrote suicide notes, took 28 Elavil tablets, normally a lethal dose, and injected herself with enough undiluted potassium chloride to kill five people. The Elavil took effect, and she fell unconscious to the floor.

The next day, she was discovered by her mother and rushed to the hospital. Medics later explained that she had not died because she was grossly overweight and the poison had dissipated throughout her body diluting itself in her blood.

At her June 1998 trial, Riggs contended she was not guilty by reason of insanity, blaming chronic, acute depression, but the Pulaski County jury convicted her.

During the penalty phase, Riggs would not allow attorneys to put on a defence, saying she wanted a death sentence, somebody the people in the death penalty business call a 'volunteer'. The jury obliged her wish and she was executed by lethal injection in Arkansas on May 2nd, 2000.

Riggs was the fifth woman executed in the United States since the reinstatement of the death penalty in 1976. She was also the first woman executed in Arkansas in more than 150 years.

By her own account of her life written whilst in jail, the torment of the last few years came after a lifetime of sexual abuse, depression and failed relationships. A native of Lawton, Okla., Riggs lived most of her life in Oklahoma City.

She recounted that her stepbrother sexually abused from about age 7 to 13. At 13, she wrote, she was also abused by a neighbour. Within a year, she began drinking, smoking cigarettes and marijuana. "I felt that no boy liked me because of my weight, so I became sexually promiscuous because I thought that was the only way I could have a boyfriend," she wrote.

By age 16, Riggs was pregnant, and in January 1988 she gave the baby boy up for adoption. After high school, she became a licensed practical nurse and worked part-time as a home care nurse and full-time at a Veterans Administration hospital. After dating several men, including a sailor and a bar bouncer, Riggs began a relationship with Timothy Thompson, who was stationed at Tinker Air Force Base.

In late October 1991, she learned she was pregnant again. She told Thompson about the baby the day before his discharge from the service. According to Rigg's mother, Carol Thomas of Jacksonville, Thompson at first wouldn't accept the baby as his own.

He moved back to his native Minnesota. "Chrissy's luck with men was about zero to nothing," Thomas said. Meanwhile, the pregnant woman rekindled her relationship with the sailor, Jon Riggs, while he was home on leave. "It was great," she wrote in her prison journal. "He felt the baby's first kick. As far as he was concerned, it was his baby."

The baby, Justin, was born on June 7th, 1992. His little sister would later call him Bubbie. The nickname stuck. "As I held Justin in my arms and looked into his little face, I became so scared. Would I be a good Mom? Could I give him all he needed?" Riggs wrote.

Jon Riggs eventually moved in with her, but she wrote that their relationship was troubled from the start. She became pregnant again, and the couple married in July 1993. But bitter disappointment visited again. Christina Riggs had a miscarriage on her wedding night.

The marriage teetered on the verge of divorce, and Riggs wrote that she became depressed and suicidal, partly, she says, as a result of prescribed birth control medication. A doctor prescribed the anti-depressant Prozac. But when she began to feel better, she stopped taking the drug.

Carol Thomas said her daughter confided in her about the depression, but minimized its effect. "She's always been that way. If I pushed her hard she might get mad and tell me what was going on," Thomas said. But generally Riggs kept her feelings to herself, her mother said.

In the spring of 1994, Riggs became pregnant again, and in December, Shelby Alexis Riggs was born. Her family called the child Sissie. "We were so happy. she was so beautiful. I didn't think things could get any better. Riggs wrote in the journal.

When a terrorist bomb ripped apart Oklahoma City's Murray Federal Building in April 1995, Riggs said the hospital assigned her to work at a triage station a short distance from the blast site. Defence attorneys indicated during her trial that she suffered from post-traumatic stress disorder as a result of working there. But prosecutors contended the hospital actually had no record that she actually worked in the blast zone.

In the summer of 1995, the couple decided to move to Sherwood where her mother was then living. They hoped the grandmother could help with day care. Riggs got a job at Baptist Hospital where her mother is employed as a food service worker.

Both children had health problems. Shelby had a series of serious ear infections, and Justin's attention deficit disorder and hyperactivity made him more than a handful.

Eventually, the Riggs' marriage crumbled. Christina divorced Jon Riggs and moved back to Oklahoma City after the father punched Justin in the stomach so hard that the boy required medical attention, according to court documents. Justin was crushed. "Justin would say, 'My Daddy hurt me, and then he went away,' " Thomas recalled. From then on, Riggs' difficult financial circumstances got worse.

Court documents show that child support payments from Jon Riggs came irregularly. And while she worked long hours at a new job at the Arkansas Heart Hospital and at a temporary nursing agency, her child care bills mounted. "The more you work, the more you need day care," she recalled "Then you feel bad about having them in day care."

Riggs wrote cheques that bounced. Her car registration and insurance expired. She realized she was going under financially. Riggs said. "I started out in a boat with a small hole. But the hole kept getting bigger, and no matter how hard you bail, you keep sinking," she said. "I was tired and I gave up. Suicide seemed like the only thing." Carol Thomas said she sensed something was wrong and asked her daughter what was wrong. "She'd just say she was tired and working too many hours," Thomas remembered.

On the evening of the murders Riggs wrote suicide notes to her mother and her ex-husband Jon Riggs. She took 28 Elavil tablets, normally a lethal dose, and injected herself with enough undiluted potassium chloride to kill five people. The undiluted potassium chloride burned a hole in her arm as big as a silver dollar as she lay in a stupor. After Riggs failed to show up for work the next day, Thomas telephoned her daughter's home but got no response. So she drove to her daughter's apartment and let herself in.

She found the children dead, and thought Christina Riggs was dead too. "All I could do was turn around and around and scream and holler, 'No. No. No.' ". Thomas said. "There's no way to describe how I felt." Thomas punched 911 into her cell phone. "My daughter and her babies are dead!" she cried.

Paramedics and police found Riggs barely alive and took her to the Baptist Memorial Medical Centre emergency room in North Little Rock. Doctors stabilized Riggs, and later moved her to intensive care where police, who had found the syringes and the suicide notes, kept her under guard.

Without allowing her attorney's to continue the appeals process after the death sentence given to her at her June 1998 trial and the legal appeal following that affirmed the sentence Riggs was executed just under two years later on May 2nd, 2000. Arkansas State governor Mike Huckabee did review the case although no request for clemency was given. He declined to intervene.

This time the poison used at the execution did work as the prison medical staff weigh the condemned to estimate the correct amount to be injected to cause death for their body weight.

END

Thank you for buying or borrowing this book. To keep up with my new releases and other information on my talks, what book festivals I am attending and other useless information about me please check out my Barry Faulkner Facebook page. I don't have a website, not enough time, but all my books, true crime, crime fiction and thrillers are on the Barry Faulkner Amazon page for the country you are in together with the first pages of each as a taster. You can also order them at your local library or book shop if they don't have them already.

DCS Palmer books (crime fiction)

Future Riches

The Felt Tip Murders

Killer is Calling

Poetic Justice

Loot

I'm With The Band

Burning Ambition

Take Away Terror

Ministry of Death

The Bodybuilder

Succession

The Black Rose

Laptops Can Kill

Screen 4

Underneath The Arches

Numbers

Ben Nevis and the Gold Digger Series

(PE thrillers)

Turkish Delight

National Treasure

Chinese Takeaway

Double Trouble

The Pyramid

True Crime Series

London Crime 1930s-2021 (factual)

UK Serial Killers 1930-2021 (factual)

UK Killers Vol. 1. A to E. 1900-1921 (factual)

UK Killers Vol. 2. F to M. 1900- 2021 (factual)

UK Killers Vol. 3. N to Z 1900-2021 (factual)

****

USA Killers Vol. 1. Alabama (factual)

USA Killers Vol..2   Arizona A to L (factual)

USA KILLERS Vol.3 Arizona M to Z plus The Ladies.

(factual)

Others

Bidder Beware (Comedy crime)

Fred Karno (biography